SPILLING THE TEA

SPILLING THE TEA

REVIVING AN ANCIENT ART
FOR A NEW GENERATION

HANNAH EVERETT

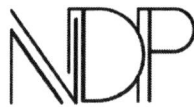

NEW DEGREE PRESS

SPILLING THE TEA

Reviving an Ancient Art for a New Generation

ISBN   978-1-64137-064-6   *Paperback*

ISBN   978-1-64137-065-3   *Ebook*

To all my friends that enjoy tea time—
I couldn't have done it without you.

CONTENTS

INTRODUCTION

———

In the US, for example, more people are drinking tea, with tea shops popping up nationwide.

—REBECCA GREENFIELD OF THE *FINANCIAL TIMES*

When the British talk about drinking tea, they rarely use the verb "drink."

It's normal that we might say, "Come over to drink tea with us."

But across the pond, that's not how it works.

While I was visiting England with a friend, we stayed with her grandma, who we affectionately called "Ouma." Every afternoon, she would "take" tea with us. She would always correct us for using the verb "drink" instead of "take."

For the British, *taking* tea is an experience. You don't sit down at afternoon tea just to drink tea. You sit down at afternoon tea to experience it.

If it's a fancy afternoon tea, you may be experiencing the subtle flavors of a rare Earl Grey tea or a Rooibos tea imported from South Africa. If it's a casual afternoon tea, like we took at Ouma's cottage in England, you may be sharing experiences from your different worlds.

During tea times, Ouma would share her worldly travel experiences with us. She'd tell us of her travels to India with her friends and of wild safaris in Kenya. In exchange, we'd share the American high school experience by teaching her slang words, like "YOLO" or "slay."

Just like life, tea is a matter of experience.

*   *

Tea is an old commodity, rooted deeply in history. And according to the Tea Association of the U.S.A., we can expect tea to remain "on the front burner for years to come" due to steady growth.

However, the tea industry is being disrupted by new forces. A product that has remained largely unchanged for many years is finally changing. The tea industry has always been somewhat dynamic due to changes in the global economy such as rising and falling demand, changing costs, politics and war, and emerging markets. Today, however, consumer behavior is the driving force for change in the tea industry. Consumers are demanding higher quality, new flavors, and industry innovation like never before—and tea is finally catching up.

We are seeing the rise of the conscious consumer thanks to innovations like the Internet that provide for greater transparency in products and value chains for commodities. Henrietta Lovell of Rare Tea Company told World of Tea, "real change is starting to happen as customers—especially online where they expect clear, transparent company information—dig deeper into where their tea comes from; who grows it, crafts it and what is the impact of the tea trade on their lives."

Consumers are also demanding better flavors. Lovell notes, cheap tea bags made by "highly industrialized farming and bulk machine processing" will no longer suffice. Specialty tea companies focus on craft to produce better tasting teas— and it's working. According to the Financial Times, "there is a growing willingness among tea drinkers to pay more for specialty teas. In the US, for example, more people are drinking tea, with tea shops popping up nationwide."

With the rise of these smaller tea companies focused on quality, the giants of the tea industry must fight back. Nigel Melican, managing director of Teacraft Ltd and executive director of Nothing But Tea Ltd, told World of Tea, "there will be a move towards bringing the economy of scale into specialty tea production without losing the 'special' appeal. Success scaling up artisanal manufacturing into business-sized units depends primarily on shortening the value chain—by direct selling to retail or at least by reducing the middleman's cut."

The industry is also seeing a shuffling of quality tea companies, like Tazo and Teavana, through acquisitions between consumer packaged goods giant Unilever and java giant Starbucks, in an attempt to snatch this growing tea segment. In December of 2012, Starbucks acquired the Teavana brand. Now, they are scheduled to shut down all Teavana mall store fronts. However, they have began to repurpose the brand as their main tea brand served in Starbucks locations across the globe. In addition, Starbucks has heavily developed their ready to drink (RTD) tea beverages, or bottled tea with the Teavana brand. In the midst of repurposing the Teavana brand, Starbucks has sold their Tazo brand to Unilever in the fall of 2017.

In addition to the rise of smaller tea companies, consumers are interested in the health benefits of tea. Emily Erb, author of blog "Leaves&Flowers," told World of Tea that she has "seen a lot more people become interested in tea in the past few years. I think people are now seeking to incorporate tea into their daily lives as a 'wellness' aid, now that it's widely known that tea is high in antioxidants and herbal infusions have a number of health benefits."

Lastly, millennials have been demanding innovations in food, and tea must step up to the plate. Following innovations in food, like a renewed focus on aesthetics, health benefits, or sustainability, tea is evolving by incorporating new trends, like cold brewing or tea-based cocktails.

All of these changes in the tea industry are a part of what experts call "third wave tea." Third wave tea means that newer, smaller tea companies are redefining how we consume tea: focusing on the quality, process, and experience of drinking tea.

Third wave tea is a phenomenon that parallels the rise of third wave coffee. If brewing a pot of Folger's coffee in your home is first wave coffee, then Starbucks is second wave coffee. Starbucks made coffee popular with espresso drinks that taste good with added syrups and milks and accessible with the pervasiveness of its locations. Finally, third wave coffee is that hipster, millennial-filled shop on your street corner that charges you $5 for the world's smallest latte. They focus on the process of making coffee and returning to the goodness of simple ingredients.

Third wave tea parallels coffee's evolution in waves. Many tea trends now focus on the origin of the tea leaves or the process of making the tea. Sometimes, they even focus on new ingredients that are added to tea to enrich the flavor.

With all the fuss about third wave tea, it seems as though real change is sweeping the industry. Yet, there are still notable critics, such as Sebastian Beckwith, founder of In Pursuit of Tea, a tea supplier to restaurants and cafes in New York. Described by *Fast Company* as a man whose "career could be its own Dos Equis commercial," Beckwith has a long and well-regarded history in the tea industry. He is a huge skeptic of this tea revival, claiming that "tea goes in waves." He claims that "if you look back on the history of tea, it's probably the one hundredth third wave of tea." Beckwith thinks that interest comes and goes along with new innovations and changes.

But there is no doubt that the tea industry is here to stay. The tea industry as a whole is valued at a whopping $10 billion. When compared to the coffee industry's valuation at $30 billion, tea is only a third of the size, but tea consumption in the United States has increased around 20 percent since 2000. Tea has always been a global commodity and the industry is in no danger of dying.

The problem is how long this "third wave" of tea will last.

If Beckwith is correct that waves of tea come and go, what can tea industry experts do to ensure this wave will stick?

A key to prolonging this "third wave" of tea is by honoring tea as more than the leaves we steep. To ride this "third wave" much longer than destined, we should look at tea as an experience.

*   *

My obsession with tea started when my family and I visited the city of Hangzhou and toured tea plantations during a two-week tour of China. I became inspired by how they made hot green tea taste so sweet and refreshing, even though it was so hot and humid outside. I used to associate green tea with a certain bitter flavor, but after this trip through China, my eyes were opened to the great flavors of all types of tea.

My obsession with tea deepened when my friends and I began a tradition we like to call Tea Night. It all started very organically, as a few of us enjoy drinking tea and began sitting down about once a week to have tea and talk.

Tea Nights are a time for all of us to slow down, put away our work, stop constantly checking our phones, and connect with life again. Taking tea for us is not about the health benefits or a boost of caffeine. While those aspects are nice, it's all about the chance to slow down and reflect or reconnect with life. Realizing why I enjoyed these Tea Nights was a pivotal point for me in deciding to write this book. Although my appreciation for tea began through my travels, my real love for tea stemmed from this deeper exploration of tea time as a time for reflection on everyday life. This idea that tea can be a time to relax and take a break from the world feeds into the realization that at its essence, tea is an experience.

*   *

In this book, you will learn about individual experiences with tea and how tea companies can prolong the third wave of tea in all tea categories to ensure a prosperous future for the industry. In addition, at the end of each chapter, I've included a tea recipe inspired by a character, place, or idea in the chapter. Each of these recipes includes a brief background or history of the type of tea and the ideal ways to prepare it.

In this book you'll meet Mrs. Raj, who will tell us stories of her native India's chai tea. You'll also meet Jawed, this avid tea drinker from Afghanistan, whose brilliant stories connect tea with hospitality. Alex, from Las Vegas, a tea lover, will show us her emotional journey through tea. You will even learn more about Ouma, the eclectic British grandmother with a zest for proper British tea time.

You will learn about innovative tea companies like Rishi Tea that focus in on serving up quality blends in an accessible way. Representatives from Rishi Tea will describe how they have spread their tea far and wide across the United States. You will learn about how to experience tea in new ways and see tea in a new light through thrilling narratives of travel all across the globe, business conquest, and inspirational icons of the tea industry, like Steven Smith.

In the following chapters, I'll share my own story of how talking over tea with my friends became a way to deepen relationships, slow down, and ultimately take time to experience life.

Maybe this will inspire you to *experience* your own Tea Night soon.

CHAPTER 1

AN EXPERIENCE

For me, tea is an experience to be cherished. Tea is a way to slow down.

The possibility of dying alone is ever-present. I learned this in September of 2017 at a Tea Night. It was a classic Sunday night. My friend Alex and I were finishing up homework and so we shot out a group text inviting our friends Karo, Field, and David over to her apartment for tea. Of course, our friend Field, (yes, like a corn field and yes, he's from Oklahoma) made an appearance to talk about his girl problems or lack thereof.

He started with the typical monologue of "I will never find a girl. I don't like going to bars and clubs to meet people. What should I do?!" But then, something amazing happened.

He stopped midsentence and said, "Did I ever tell you about the time I almost died this summer?"

Immediately, Alex said, "No. Oh my gosh, Field, what happened?" And he began...

"So I realized the possibility of dying alone is ever-present. And I came to this realization after I almost died eating a burrito this summer. Alone. At the age of 20. In my friend's kitchen. Without (him or) his family there. Or my family there.

"It was a Friday evening, I got off work. I went to Chipotle and I was excited. I had the house to myself this weekend. And I decided to get a huge burrito, and it wasn't just a burrito. It was a quesarito, which is a quesadilla used as a tortilla for a burrito. So, it's really like two meals. It's like eating a baby— it's literally like six pounds."

"I was so excited to eat it when I got to my friend's house where I was staying that I just took a huge bite and I didn't chew it."

"I started choking at his breakfast table, and then I realized, mid-choke, I was completely alone. And would be completely alone for the next two days because my friend's parents were out of town. So, this could be it. And I don't wanna die in my friend's kitchen and have my friend's parents walk in Sunday evening to my corpse—my cold, hard corpse on their kitchen floor.

"I stood up out of my chair. My face became flushed and eventually, I mustered up the strength to hoist up the said quesadilla piece out of my throat to dislodge it. I took a few breaths and proceeded to finish the quesarito safely."

After he finished this story, we all sat there, and I thought to myself, "What the heck? This is hilarious, but what the heck?"

We all broke out in laughter and started poking fun at Field. But still curious about why he decided to tell us this, I asked, "Field, what does this have to do with you not having a girl-friend? Why'd you feel the need to tell us this story?"

"Well, it made me realize my life could end at any moment," said Field.

"So you're telling me this is a roundabout way of making a point that if you had a girlfriend to eat with, you wouldn't have choked. Or she could have saved you from choking?" I said.

"Um, I don't know if it was as much as she could have saved me. Because obviously I am capable of saving myself. 'Cause I did. 'Cause I'm a stud. But, the idea of not being able to experience life. You get a perspective of 'I could get a life-changing diagnosis at any moment; I could choke on a burrito.' And it makes experiencing life that much more important."

Alex butted in and asked, "So how close were you to really dying?"

Field responds, "I'd be lying if I didn't say this was embellished a little bit, but the threat was there. Had I chosen not to do anything about it, I would not be here today. I could have just let the burrito take its course."

"But seriously, this story was just a realization that it could end at any moment in the most awkward way. Just not the way you wanna go out. Like, there are definitely other ways I'd like to die."

Ah, Field . . .

*   *

As hilarious as Field's story is, there is a lesson to be learned. Like Field said, life is about experiencing things. And when Field's quesarito threatened to cut his life short, Field learned to truly value his experiences. Sure, Field hasn't done anything great yet (sorry, Field), but one day, he will. And each one of his experiences up to this point will only build to his future. Field didn't want his life, his experiences, to be cut short by a burrito.

Had Alex and I not decided to invite a few friends over to our place for our regular tea drinking ritual, I might never have heard Field's barely near-death experience.

I also wouldn't have reflected about the deeper meaning of his story.

All thanks to afternoon tea with friends.

As Field shared with us, life is truly about enjoying experiences. And I like to believe we should understand tea in the same way.

*   *

I began writing this book with only my own experiences with tea to guide me. My "tea experiences" were very narrow, limited to a few tea cultures and my finite knowledge of the details of making tea. But through interviewing tea lovers, tea experts, and industry leaders, I have learned so much: I have learned about the British Tea Council's attempt to increase tea consumption in the United States, I have learned about how all tea technically comes from one plant (the *Camellia sinensis*), and I have learned that the United States' beloved iced tea was actually invented in the North (not the South).

However, what struck me most about my research is how much I have learned from non-experts on the topic. These are the people who may not have any experience in the industry, but have day-to-day contact with tea or come from countries with very established tea cultures.

With these interviews, I was able to dive into how and why people really consume tea. I still do not know everything there is to know about tea and will not pretend to. But what I aim to do with this book is inform you—you tea lover or hater, amateur or expert—about my findings.

And one of my biggest findings is that tea is all about experiences. Despite the fact that all tea comes from one tea plant, there are many varieties with different flavors depending on growing process and preparation. Adding herbal ingredients can also create new flavor blends. Our experiences with tea can even change depending on how we consume it: we can sample tea in a tea shop or take it at home with friends, we can enjoy iced tea, scalding hot tea, or a tall tea-based cocktail spiked with our favorite bourbon.

This book highlights how individuals experience tea and how businesses help create and enable those experiences. Although people commonly drink tea for its health benefits or caffeine content, in the stories and examples I highlight in this book, you will find one theme that unites them all: tea as a way to experience life in and of itself. Tea is more than the leaves we steep.

*   *

Many people see coffee as the biggest competitor to tea. This misconception is especially prevalent in the United States, where many of us have a morning coffee ritual. Even I need a cup of some sort of coffee every morning to function. But tea is not necessarily a substitute for coffee. Unlike coffee, tea is not directly vital for my survival throughout the day. I literally depend on my cup of coffee because I'm addicted to the high caffeine content. But, I still drink tea! Tea offers a different experience: It allows me to slow down and reflect.

As highlighted by my Tea Nights with friends, tea offers us the chance to slow down in a way that other beverages cannot. Coffee is very utilitarian. We take it to wake up in the morning, get through long afternoons at work, or power through a paper late at night. Coffee is often taken on the go, in a hurry. Tea, on the other hand, is more often a ritual. Tea rituals may be more common across the globe in other cultures, but in writing this book, I also found them here in the United States.

*   *

JASMINE TEA

Jasmine tea is an herbal tea, meaning it's not made from the tea plant *Camellia sinensis*. In fact, all types of tea—such as white tea, black tea, or green tea—comes from this plant. Other teas that are "herbal" come from other plants or spices.

Jasmine tea is a favorite among my friends. My roommate Angela and friend Alex absolutely adore jasmine tea. Alex has always loved jasmine tea (as you will hear about later), but Angela hasn't always liked tea. In fact, she came to like jasmine tea in a roundabout way.

In her freshman year of college, Angela was doing well; she was having a great time. The first few weeks of freshman year, she was thriving. But this didn't last, as she began to enter a dark period: midterms. Angela was lost and all alone; she had nowhere to turn. Angela needed a friend and that friend was caffeine.

As someone who had said, "I will hate coffee 'til the day I die," clearly the magical roasted beans were not an option for Angela. She thought back to her high school days, when her best friend Charles would order chai lattes from Starbucks every day. She reasoned, "Why not? I'm desperate. I'll try almost anything."

Angela got up from her table in the library, walked to Midnight Mug, the coffee shop, and ordered a chai latte. She took a sip and something magical happened—Angela's whole body perked up. She got the energy she needed to last through the night. Her productivity went through the roof!

After a few weeks of nonstop chai lattes and powering through one midterm after the other, Angela realized how many calories and how much sugar was in one chai latte. Plus, her body was always too jittery. She needed to cut caffeine out of her life. Although the chai had provided a boost for her during midterms, she no longer needed all that caffeine. But she really liked the idea of drinking tea.

Luckily, Angela found out that herbal teas often have low levels of caffeine and taste just as sweet as her chai, without all the sugar. And one of her favorites was jasmine tea.

While it took Angela becoming addicted to the caffeine in chai to turn to the low-caffeine option of jasmine tea, Alex has always been a fan and loves jasmine blossom tea.

Jasmine tea is often made of a green or white tea base. These tea leaves are infused with the scents of the jasmine flower to give the tea a sweeter taste.

However, jasmine blossom teas also contain the actual jasmine flower blossom. This tea is literally just the jasmine flower. It comes in a little package and looks like a little ball. When you add hot water to steep the tea, the little ball opens up to reveal a beautiful jasmine flower.

Typically, the best temperature to steep any jasmine tea is around 160 to 180 degrees Fahrenheit, a little cooler than other teas. This is one of the most beautiful teas, and it is served best in clear tea glasses, so you can see all of the beauty!

CHAPTER 2

'OH THE SEVENTH CUP'

———

The first cup kisses away my thirst,
and my loneliness is quelled by the second.
The third gives insight worthy of ancient scrolls,
and the fourth exiles my troubles.
My body becomes lighter with the fifth,
and the sixth sends word from immortals.
*But the seventh—**oh the seventh cup**—if I drink you,*
a wind will hurry my wings toward the sacred island.

—LUTONG (795-835 A.D.), TRANS. CHRISTOPHER NELSON

"In India, tea is very big. But it's the most popular in the north because it's grown there," said Mrs. Raj.

Mrs. Raj grew up in India in a big, relatively well-off Indian family. She left home to go to university in the United States to find better opportunity. She brought her passion, desire to learn, and tenacity to the United States, specifically to the suburbs of Chicago, where she has raised a wonderful, talented family. But that's not all she brought from India. She also brought along her love for tea, chai tea.

Mrs. Raj continued, "Assam and Darjeeling in northern India account for most of the country's tea production." Assam, a region in India known for its black teas, produces over 55 percent of India's tea every year, according to Rate Tea. Darjeeling is also known for its black teas, but has begun producing more green, white, and even oolong teas in the past few years.

"In India, we don't really drink green tea. We always drink black tea with milk and sugar," added Mrs. Raj. As it's largest tea production regions specialize in black tea, India has a strong taste for black tea.

A variety of the tea plant has always been native to India. The India Brand Equity Foundation noted that before British colonization, Indian people drank and used tea leaves as early as 750 B.C.

After the British developed a taste for black tea through Chinese imports, they wanted to cultivate their own tea to avoid importing tea from China. So, the British stole tea plant seeds from China and attempted to grow the leaves in India, one of their colonies.

The climate in India was not right for the Chinese tea plant and so the British failed to cultivate tea. However, according to the India Brand Equity Foundation, a British botanist discovered a variation of the Chinese tea plant in India being cultivated by the local Singhpho tribe. With this variation of the Chinese tea plant, the British began cultivating their own tea. In 1835, British businessmen set up the first Western tea plantations in Assam, India.

The British tea plantations in India started to produce decent tea leaves. Soon enough, the British no longer had to import tea from China. By shifting tea production to their colonies in India and even West Africa, the British were able to dominate global tea trade. "By 1853, India's tea exports had reached 183.4 tons," according to the India Brand Equity Foundation. Tea production and consumption in the British empire was felt across the globe.

While the British simply produced varieties of black tea to export to England and their other colonies, India has a special tradition that makes their black tea distinct from British black tea. This Indian black tea is known as masala chai and is very important to India. Mrs. Raj's stories of drinking masala chai back home in India perfectly highlight this beverage's influence.

In the past decade or so, chai tea has become a phenomenon in the United States due to coffee giant Starbucks. While chai tea has always been a nationally consumed drink in India and many other countries in the world, Starbucks helped an Indian-inspired version of the drink become popular in the United States.

Mrs. Raj described spiced chai tea as "a black tea with added spices—like ginger, cardamon, and cloves." In India, spiced chai is called masala chai and has its origins as an herbal blend. According to TheSpruce.com, masala chai "is steeped in tales of royalty and herbal medicine and has evolved over the years to include countless variations and a worldwide fan base." Chai was originally a drink without any tea leaves, meant to be a herbal remedy. Later, black tea leaves were added to the mix.

Mrs. Raj noted that back home, families would make their own masala chai, adding different proportions of spices. "Chai is freshly ground in each house and prepared differently by each household." She said that at her home in India, "we always offer guests water, then followed by tea."

Chai is also served outside of the home in India. "On the streets of India, there are little tea shops on the side of the road," said Mrs. Raj as she described the way tea is prepared at tea stalls. Everyone in India takes tea breaks during the work day. They head outside, find a tea stall, and drink their tea no matter the weather. Today, masala chai is always served hot in India, even during the warmer months.

She noted the distinct way that chai is brewed. Instead of steeping the tea and herbal spices in water and then adding milk, the milk is boiled with the tea. Mrs. Raj said this is because "the street stalls that sell tea use unpasteurized milk. So, they must boil the milk with the rest of the tea."

Masala chai is deeply ingrained in Indian culture. With innovations in the food industry, companies are even creating masala chai powdered packets for tea on the go. "Companies are making tea sachets (tea bags) with milk powder and sugar," said Mrs. Raj.

But not everyone is pleased with this change. Chetan Bhagat, a blogger for the Times of India, is upset with the lack of quality of these packets.

"Ask any Indian how he or she likes his or her tea," Bhagat wrote in a post. "They will tell you chai has to be brewed and boiled for a few minutes with water and a small amount of milk. Sounds simple enough, isn't it?"

"No sir. Go to any airport in the country, and try to get a cup of tea like you make at home. You won't get it. Instead, what you will get is a disgusting, synthetic version. It will contain coagulated milk powder and a tea bag with an ugly thread hanging out."

In this somewhat comedic article, it's clear that Bhagat prefers the homemade method. However, Bhagat gets serious when he calls this a national crisis.

"Indians don't just love tea; they can't live without it. Tea for Indians is like blood or hormones or enzymes or whatever fluid your body needs to function."

Bhagat went further to call the use of coagulated milk powder and tea bags a "matter of national shame." If "America runs on Dunkin," then India runs on masala chai.

Whether or not you agree with Bhagat, it's clear that tea is a key facet of Indian culture and has permeated every part of Indian life. From noting common places, like the airport to the office, as places these "horrible" tea packets are consumed, Bhagat makes an interesting point. In the United States, we tend to associate tea with a fancy, British tea time reserved for wealthy elites. However, in places like India, tea is part of everyday life. Tea isn't just for the wealthy who have hours to spend on a fancy tea time. Tea is a way of life.

Tea is also a way of pausing. Mrs. Raj said that going to the tea stalls serves as "a break for office workers during the lunch hour or midmorning." Even though she notes that these small breaks can be very quick, sometimes only five minutes, it is still a way for workers to take a break and get out of the office. "We've learned to drink hot tea pretty quickly," Mrs. Raj joked.

From Mrs. Raj's explanation of tea in India, it's clear that tea has an important place in the everyday lives of the people. Maybe it's because India produces a lot of tea and its production is so engrained in its history. But maybe it's because the spices added to masala chai taste so much better than our Lipton tea bags. Either way, the cultural differences are striking.

In his article, Bhagat said Indians "can't live without their tea," alluding to the need for caffeine. He noted that "the thousands of groggy-eyed people at any airport every morning" need their tea for energy. He went on to say, "as they take those godforsaken early morning flights, they beg for tea."

It's clear the caffeine and energy derived from tea is a big factor of tea's success in India. However, as Mrs. Raj noted, taking tea serves as an important break time for the working class. The tea stalls that line the streets are a safe haven from office politics and the chaos of a stressful workday. Tea is not only to get you going, but also to get you to stop, slow down, and take a break.

* *

Hearing Mrs. Raj talk about her experiences with tea reminded me of how one of my good friends, Alex Rimoldi, started enjoying tea.

Alex's family is obsessive about coffee—they have a full-scale Marzocco espresso machine. Her brother and father make shots of espresso, cappuccinos, and lattes all day long. Bu Alex doesn't get the big whoop about coffee—to her, it's just dirt in a cup.

Alex's first memory of tea is from all the way back when she was in elementary school. Her babysitter would always offer her and her little brother hot Lipton tea with a little bit of milk and a Milky Way candy bar on the side. Alex was too little to remember why her babysitter liked tea, but she remembers that the sitter always offered to share with the kids.

Alex does remember when she started to like tea herself, though. In early middle school, Alex and her mom started taking tea before bed. Alex would always drink a cup of jasmine tea to help her calm down before getting some shut-eye. It became a nightly routine for Alex and Mrs. Rimoldi. They used it as a time to relax and talk together.

Alex is super close and connected with her family. My family and I are close, but the frequency that Alex stays in touch with her family shocks me. (Sorry I don't call you as often as

I should, Mom!) Today, Alex goes to college on the east coast in Washington, D.C., and her parents are still back home in Las Vegas. Despite the distance, Alex is always on the phone with her mom or her brother. Even if she's had a few drinks at happy hour, if she needs her mom Kirsten, she does not hesitate to hop on the line. Despite her dad's busy schedule as a doctor, he still finds time to come visit her. Her parents never shy away from giving her relationship advice. Her dad, Ren, always tells her that she should not have to settle!

Alex also talks to her brother, who is now a sophomore at Syracuse University, almost every day. They talk about how school is going, the stressfulness of finding a job, and how her brother should not join a fraternity. After the Las Vegas shooting on October 1st of 2017, her family's closeness was on full display. Although no one she knew was killed, Alex could not help but feel hit hard by the bad news. I remember her rolling up to our 10 a.m. class with large, mirrored aviator glasses on, hiding her puffy eyes.

The first thing Alex did that morning was call her father because she knew that as a doctor, he would be seeing some of the injuries. She just wanted to be there for him and make sure everything at his work was okay. Alex also called her brother; she found solace in the fact that he too was feeling horrible that day, even though they did not know anyone who was killed.

Alex's closeness with her family might just be part of their Italian heritage. But I also think this closeness is partly attributed, if not simply evident, in Alex's tea time with her mother in middle school. After establishing that jasmine tea bedtime ritual with Kirsten, the whole family got in on the tradition. Her younger brother even got Alex a fancy tea set for Christmas one year.

Although she could not talk much about the origins of tea or detail every single flavor profile out there, Alex can tell you one of the most important things about tea: that tea is not only a means for experiencing beautiful, exotic flavors, but is also a way to slow down and reconnect with her family. Alex says that tea gives her space to be "vulnerable and open to others, to express diverse opinions, and to show others you care." Not only does tea allow her to pause her life, it also allows her to reflect.

*   *

Alex brought her love for tea to Georgetown University during her sophomore year.

I am a student at Georgetown University, and like all other students here, I live in my own self-inflected pressure cooker. Naturally, I needed to find a healthy release from all this stress that did not involve substance abuse. Luckily, sophomore year brought Alex and Alex brought Tea Night. At first I couldn't really remember how tea time at Georgetown became a thing with my friends, but luckily, Alex was able to shine some light on the topic and remind me of the origins of our now-sacred tradition.

But first, a little background. I met all my friends who participate in Tea Night while I studied abroad in Hong Kong after freshman year. David, Alex, Bridget, Karolina, Field, and I decided to continue our friendship post-Hong Kong. In fact, I even spent one of the last few weeks of that summer visiting Bridget on Long Island, New York.

One of the first things I did once everyone moved back to campus was visit Bridget—who was also my roommate in Hong Kong—while she was moving into her dorm. I ran into her parents, Dan and Jackie, in the elevator and helped them carry things up to Bridget's room. While we were riding in the elevator, we stopped on the second floor and to my surprise, Field got on! Field didn't know Bridget's parents, but he said "hi" to me and began saying, "and hello Mr. and Mrs. Everett, nice to meet you . . . " not realizing they were Bridget's parents. And after that awkward but funny encounter, we all established that our Hong Kong squad would continue to be friends on the Hilltop.

As college friends do, we hung out in each other's dorms. But Alex had an apartment, so we often found ourselves crashing her place because she had a living room. When you happen to be at Alex's, you also happen to be offered tea. All of this friendship and tea drinking happened very organically, and eventually, a pattern developed.

Tea night became Tea Night™ all thanks to matcha tea. It was a Friday night and as college students, Karolina and I were most definitely going out. However, Bridget Bingham is not your typical college student. On this Friday night, Bridget Bingham wanted, no, *needed* matcha tea. She rummaged through her food shelves and in the way back corner, found a small package of matcha powder she got at the end of the summer. Just as she thought she was about to quench her desire for matcha, she realized that she didn't have the proper tools to enjoy it—a tea cup and a whisk. She immediately called Alex. Alex had tea cups but no whisk, but told Bridget to come to her apartment anyway because she was planning to stay in and wanted a relaxing Friday night. So Bridget packed up her matcha and headed over.

On the way to Alex's apartment, Bridget had a brilliant idea— David may have just what she needs. She dialed his number and asked if he has a whisk for matcha. Now, David is a perfect boy. David is the type of boy you introduce to your parents as your boyfriend even though he's not just because they are dropping too many hints and think there is something wrong with you. And because David is a perfect boy, David obviously has a matcha whisk. Instead of searching for a bottle of vodka on a Friday night, my friends were searching for all the tools necessary to make an authentic cup of matcha.

As Alex was explaining all of this to me, she named it the Matcha Effect. She said that while our friend group happened to have tea a lot while hanging out, on this night, the purpose of our hanging out *was* tea. So, tea night became Tea Night™ thanks to Bridget's insane matcha craving.

Tea Nights are special and sacred to our friend group. They also happen very often.

- Just failed a midterm? Tea Night.
- Want to procrastinate writing a paper? Tea Night.
- Just got an interview at a bank and freaking out about it? Tea Night.
- Just got back from a night out and need to sober up before bed? Tea Night.
- Worried you're going to die alone due to a rogue burrito bite? Tea Night.

For my friends, Tea Night is a time to relax. It's a time to be vulnerable and let out your worries and emotions, happy or sad. Everyone needs a space like this to talk about their feelings, especially in high-pressure environments. And at a college like Georgetown, sometimes it can feel like there are no other places to find this relief. I am lucky enough to have found it in friends like these and Tea Nights.

As Bridget says, "Georgetown is easy to get caught up in. Tea Nights help me zoom out and get the bigger picture. Others should appreciate this time to reflect more. This does not have to be tea, but anything that gives an opportunity to reflect."

Alex echoes this sentiment, noting that Tea Nights "make her feel understood." Alex feels like she now "belongs on Georgetown's campus; I've realized I now have friends for life," all because tea brought us closer. Something about the warmth or the comforting flavors makes people open up.

For us, Tea Nights encompass the concept of taking a break from it all and slowing down. Although they may not be as quick or as often as the 5-minute tea breaks during the busy work day that Mrs. Raj described, the principle of taking a break and slowing down is similar.

The Tea Nights I described above include more of an emotional aspect to tea than Mrs. Raj touched on. However, that doesn't mean that tea is not emotional in India as well.

One Indian blogger describes her emotional connection to tea as nostalgic. Kena Shree, a self-proclaimed tea addict, described tea as serving an emotional purpose because for her, it is "connected to so many memories and narratives." In her blog published on the *Huffington Post*, she notes specific experiences of tea from her mom preparing it in the morning to tea being served on the railway to not being allowed to have tea as a child. In her adult life, she says having five cups of chai a day helps her stay connected to these memories. Tea helps Shree slow down and reconnect with her memories.

One day, I hope tea will do the same for me. Though I grew up in a family without tea traditions, my travels have inspired me to become a tea drinker and Tea Nights with my friends have helped me create memories. I too may have a nostalgic connection to tea one day.

* *

This emotional connection to tea is nothing new.

Have you ever wanted to get something off your chest but had no one to talk to? Well, as of 2015, there's an app for that. Some critics may argue that technology is no replacement for sound mental health advice, but that's not the point of listening app 7 Cups of Tea.

7 Cups of Tea is a community of certified listeners that provides users a place to vent. Certified listeners aren't trained professionals, but they don't need to be to simply listen to others' problems. CEO Glen Moriarty launched the app back in 2015 when he realized that because he and his wife were trained psychologists, they always had someone to turn to for venting purposes. However, he realized that others may not have this same liberty. Thus, 7 Cups of Tea was born.

Launched in Y Combinator—a U.S. startup accelerator—the app aims to revolutionize therapy, especially for lower level needs. Moriarty stresses that this app will never be a replacement for professional services, but it can be a tool among others in the toolbox of mental health resources.

7 Cups of Tea relies heavily on its community of listeners, who are sourced from partner mental health organizations, and can be students or even mental health professionals. Listeners go through background checks, have training opportunities, and can earn badges for successful connections. As much as the app builds a community for users, a strong sense of community is also fostered for the listeners that make the app possible.

7 Cups of Tea gets its name from a Chinese poem in which each cup of tea provides a unique sense of emotional healing. The poem goes:

The first cup kisses away my thirst,
and my loneliness is quelled by the second.
The third gives insight worthy of ancient scrolls,
and the fourth exiles my troubles.
My body becomes lighter with the fifth,
and the sixth sends word from immortals.
*But the seventh—**oh the seventh cup**—if I drink you,*
a wind will hurry my wings toward the sacred island.

—LUTONG (795-835 A.D.), TRANS. CHRISTOPHER NELSON

In the poem, physical needs, like thirst are met. But far more important, emotional needs are relieved.

The reason this 7 Cups of Tea app caught my eye is because it frames tea in an emotional light. Compared to coffee, tea's associations are more often rooted in emotional relief. Tea is often taken while sitting down and relaxing, while coffee is taken to go or as an energizer on the way to work.

Especially in American culture, you don't often hear about people having their daily morning tea. It's their morning coffee. There are even coffee cups that say "Don't talk to me until I've had my coffee" that poke fun of this ritual. While morning coffee is rooted in finding energy for the day, tea can be taken in the morning, afternoon, or night.

Let's consider afternoon tea. When I hear afternoon tea, I immediately think of the queen of England hobnobbing over tea with other royal court members. They gossip, talk politics, and enjoy each others' company. Imagine trying to do this every day with your morning coffee before work. It just wouldn't happen.

Tea culture is simply slower than the morning coffee culture in the United States. One of my fellow students, Brittany, told me about this phenomenon when she heard about my book. Brittany studied abroad in Strasbourg, France, last semester and said that the city was full of cute little tea shops. She notes, "I have such good memories of sitting down with friends and just chatting for an hour over a cup of tea and a small pastry, and it was such a nice social event." Americans just don't make time for these activities as much as other cultures.

Tea is an important conduit to slowing down, taking time to gather together and listen, and expressing feelings. Like the 7 Cups of Tea app, gathering together over cups of tea serves as an emotional and stress release.

Each line of the poem explains how each cup of tea addresses a different need. The poem expresses many of the needs I find satisfied by having a cup of tea with friends during Tea Nights. It is because of these emotions expressed the poem that I became interested the experience of drinking tea.

* *

MRS. RAJ'S CHAI TEA

In honor of taking a break, this chapter's recipe is Mrs. Raj's traditional Indian chai tea (not your average Starbucks chai latte). Although Mrs. Raj described quick breaks with chai tea in India, this recipe will take you a little longer to make, unless you've got a tea stall right outside your office with chai tea on tap!

Here's the ingredient list for one cup of tea:

- A small pot
- 3/4 cup milk
- 1/4 cup water
- 1 teaspoon sugar
- 1 slightly heaped teaspoon of good quality loose black tea leaves
- 2 cardamom pods

Mrs. Raj says to "slightly crush the cardamom" in the bottom of the pot, so that the full flavors come out. Then pour in the "milk and water and place on medium heat. Next, add the sugar."

"When the milk is close to a boil, lower the heat and add the tea leaves and stir a few times. Allow this mixture to boil for 20 or 30 seconds and remove from heat."

It's important to not let this tea mixture boil for too long "as it will leave a bitter taste." Finally, "strain and pour in serving mug."

CHAPTER 3

PUTTING THE 'TEA' IN HOSPITALITY

———

In Afghanistan, people rarely use tea bags because one, they are more expensive and two, people drink from big tea kettles, so loose leaf is easier. Tea bags are made for one cup. People don't drink by cups in Afghanistan, they drink by big kettles. We've got big families; there are like 10 kids. And if everyone wants three cups of tea . . . you do the math.

—JAWED

When you think of the great tea countries of the world, you probably think of China, England, and India. Shockingly enough, Afghanistan imported over 10 pounds of tea per person in 2012, according to DominionTea.com. This made Afghanistan the global leader in tea imports per capita in

2012. When looking at tea import reports from the Food and Agricultural Organization of the United Nations, in 2010, their data shows Afghanistan at the top of tea imports per capita during this time, as well. Collecting data on tea imports, exports, and consumption can be difficult and somewhat inaccurate at times. And although this data on tea imports is slightly dated, it sheds light on the importance of tea in Afghanistan.

According to Dominion Tea, tea became important in Afghanistan because of its geographical location. As a trade and travel gateway between the Middle East and Asia, this country was first introduced to tea by Chinese traders.

Being from Afghanistan, Jawed's love for tea matches up with the import numbers. Jawed is a senior at Georgetown University and has brought his love for tea with him to campus.

Jawed says when he's back home, "tea is always on tap. If I'm back home, on average, I'm maybe drinking 10 to 15 cups of tea a day. And these are decent-sized cups."

When I asked him why tea was so big in Afghanistan he jokingly said, "because, there's not much to do!" But he's somewhat serious. "Even when my dad drives, he has tea. When he stops at a traffic sign, he takes a sip, then we move on!"

He stated, "It's just a big part of the culture. Even when it's 35 degrees Celsius (really hot) out, you still drink tea. Even though it's summer, people don't care! People just drink tea, all the time. There's no special occasion. You have it before meals, after meals. Even during meals. Imagine having soup for lunch and a cup of green tea. It's prevalent, it's present everywhere and all the time."

Other than being way more popular in Afghanistan (in the United States, we imported under one pound of tea per capita in 2012, compared to Afghanistan's 10 pounds, according to Dominion Tea), tea as a product is also different. Afghan tea culture is very simple and about sticking to the basics.

"In the States, you know how you have all the variety of teas, like the fruity stuff? Yeah, that's not the thing back home. Back home you either have black tea, like an English breakfast tea, or you have green tea," says Jawed. Like Jawed noted earlier, this is very different from how we sometimes have tea in the United States. We have so many different add-ins available, like flavored sweeteners. Sometimes, we even mix teas with lemonade (Starbucks' Hibiscus Tea Lemonade— shaken, not stirred).

This was a pretty striking difference. Even in other tea cultures around the world, there are some add-ins. For example, the British add milk and sugar. In India, Mrs. Raj talked about the herbal masala chai spices. I wanted to know more about how Afghans take their tea.

Jawed clarified for me and said there were a few things commonly added to tea: cardamom, sugar, and saffron, all on different occasions.

"The most common thing you would add to your tea, especially green tea, is cardamom. Cardamom is more for smell. The flavor of the tea changes slightly. But the cardamon just smells really good. The cardamom just gives it a little bounce. If that makes sense to all the tea lovers out there," joked Jawed.

Jawed mentioned that saffron was another popular, but expensive, additive. Saffron can be priced higher than gold so you only add "like one or two leaves," he explained. "If it's too strong you get a headache. You can also use saffron by itself as tea, but that's too expensive. We also use saffron for coloring our rice and other food, but we add it to tea because it relaxes you."

Saffron is a spice that looks like a pinkish leaf. It's often used in cooking. For example, saffron rice and saffron salmon are common dishes.

"If you put three or four strands in a glass, in five seconds, the water is orange yellow. Saffron tea! It's super bright and vibrant," said Jawed. He also noted that saffron is sold by the gram because it's so expensive.

"A big movement in Afghanistan these days is to get farmers to grow saffron instead of opium because it's more expensive. But war lords control the opium routes, so farmers still farm it. But it would be an amazing alternative in the warmer parts of Afghanistan."

He even said that sometimes you can get a little high from the saffron if there is too much: "You get kind of doozy. You don't wanna have too much, especially if you're on medication."

The last popular add-in Jawed mentioned was sugar, but it's only used at certain times. Jawed said, "In Afghanistan, there are not a lot of rich people. The country is very poor. So, what they do in the morning is they add sugar to their tea and eat that with a piece of bread. That's their breakfast."

Jawed explained, "You add sugar so you can have a sweeter breakfast. Afghan breakfast is so plain, it's just bread. Adding sugar to your tea gives the breakfast a little more flavor. It's like sweet tea and naan."

Afghanistan imports such a massive amount of tea per person because everyone drinks it. And for people who lead simpler lives, tea is an important part of breakfast. Adding the sugar gives everything a little more flavor and the mealtime becomes an important morning ritual.

In fact, even the people in Afghanistan who don't like tea still drink it in the morning. I asked Jawed if he knows anyone back home who doesn't like tea or doesn't drink tea. The closest example he could think of was his uncle, who still has two cups a day.

"One of my uncles doesn't like drinking tea. But he has one cup of sweet tea before breakfast and another cup of tea after breakfast to wash it down and that's it," explained Jawed.

When I questioned Jawed further about why his uncle feels the need to drink tea if he doesn't like it, Jawed responded: "He still has it in the morning for energy. It's not as much the caffeine as it is the fact that it's breakfast time. With breakfast, you just gotta have a sweet cup of tea with sugar. Dry naan by itself? No. You gotta have tea with it."

I asked Jawed about the caffeine content of tea to see if he thought he was addicted. This man drinks as much as 15 cups of tea a day when he's back home. That's a crazy amount of caffeine, but Jawed said, "Maybe because I drink tea a lot, the caffeine does not do anything for me. I could be having tea and going to bed. But this is because I only have green tea."

He explained that he "had experimented between green tea and black tea. And the reason I mainly drink green tea is because I get hooked on black tea, similar to coffee." He doesn't like being dependent on tea to get going in the morning.

Jawed prefers to stick to his green tea, especially ever since he became addicted to afternoon coffee thanks to his internship in Washington, D.C., this summer. He commented, "Towards the end of the summer, especially in the afternoon, the siesta time is so real. You're in the office and you're like, 'I could use a coffee right now.' I couldn't hold off."

Tea in Afghanistan is also a lot cheaper. Jawed says you can get a kilo (2.2 pounds) for around $7, and that's the really nice stuff!

He says he buys his tea at bazaars back home. "Imagine a CVS, good sized. But all tea! There are all different types of tea between green and black. Different auras and smells, but they fall within the green or black tea category. Some already have cardamom added in, but none would have saffron because that's too expensive. There's good quality stuff, bad quality stuff. But it's all super cheap."

Tea being cheap and accessible for all Afghan people is important because they have big families who all love tea. The tea is all loose leaf, too. "People rarely use bags," Jawed explained, "because one, they are more expensive and two, people drink from big tea kettles, so loose leaf is easier. Tea bags are made for one cup. People don't drink by cups in Afghanistan, they drink by big kettles. We've got big families; there are like 10 kids. And if everyone wants three cups of tea. . . you do the math."

Tea is also an important part of Afghan celebrations. Jawed said that "during big festivals, sometimes we create a highly concentrated base and have hot water on the side. The concentrate is really bitter, but we just pour hot water over it. If you have a lot of people, you don't have to make a super big tea kettle. You just add hot water. You can tell the difference, but no one cares. It's more for efficiency."

*   *

After talking to Jawed, it was clear his home country was steeped in tea. However, there is more to the story of tea in Afghanistan. One of the reasons it is so prevalent is because of the strong sense of hospitality in Afghan culture.

The blog "About Afghanistan" mentioned a story often told to young people in Afghanistan to acquaint them with the idea of hospitality:

> A group of thieves one night entered a man's house while all of the family was asleep. The thieves, under the instructions

of their leader, began carrying out carpets and cushions—anything portable that had any worth. In the dark, the leader of the band reached into a cupboard, finding a hard smooth rock-like object. He immediately decided that it must be some kind of a gem. The thieves had almost finished their work when the leader put this 'gem' to his lips. Tasting it, he was not only disappointed at finding that the gem was just a block of salt, but he was horrified that he had stolen the property of a man whose salt he had eaten. He immediately ordered his men to return all of the property to the house before the family awoke.

In the story, the leader of the thieves accidentally has some of the salt block, which is the homeowner's food. Because the homeowner had shared his food with the leader, even unknowingly, the leader ordered all the thieves to stop robbing the home. By eating the family's food, the leader of the thieves was now indebted to the home owner; they were now friends and the leader could not wrong the homeowner like this. It would be against his honor.

Afghans take hosting guests very seriously. Sharing tea and food is a big part of hospitality there.

I came across a blog written by an American soldier in Afghanistan. The blog is called "Bill and Bob's Excellent Afghan Adventure" and describes the citizen-soldier's experiences in

Afghanistan. One of the blog entries is exclusively about tea. In this entry, the author documents all sorts of tea experiences in Afghanistan, many of them involving the overwhelming hospitality of Afghans in offering tea.

The author of these blog entries had lots of experiences meeting Afghans and discussing military business. In all these meetings, chai was served. The author stated, "More often, the offer of chai was not an obligatory gesture but a genuine expression of friendship and a desire to have relaxed conversation with another."

The offering of tea could sometimes seem ironic. In the blog post, the author talks about a friend who was offered tea in a village near where he had just been in a firefight with opposing troops. He was "quite sure that some of the people serving chai that day had been shooting at him shortly before."

During these meetings, small talk would precede any business talk. The author noted that "Afghans have a lively sense of humor and truly appreciate jokes and laughter. Very often they will poke mild fun at each other, but will not shame another man."

Tea is a space for Afghans to enjoy this humor. The author notes this, stating, "Chai is all about civil relaxation, and

Afghans *love* chai." These notes about humor check out with my friend Jawed: He's a pretty funny dude.

"Bill and Bob's Excellent Afghan Adventure," written by an American citizen-solider with 27 years of experience in Afghanistan, ends this blog post with the following statement:

> . . . Chai is more than the tea. If an Afghan ever offers you chai, take him up on it. Chai is an experience; a hospitable, civil experience that is done nearly the same way any place I went in Afghanistan. It's a distinctively Afghan experience.

*   *

Tea and hospitality in Afghanistan are greatly intertwined. Helen Saberi, author of "Tea: A Global History," said that showing hospitality to house guests is very important in Afghanistan. She wrote that "the warmth and generosity of Afghan hospitality can be almost overwhelming at times."

Saberi visited Afghanistan in 1971 where she met her husband. She has been an expat ever since. When she travels to other cities, Saberi is often a house guest at friends' homes.

Saberi wrote in her blog "Afghan Culture Unveiled":

A guest is always made to feel welcome and special. He or she will be invited to sit in the place of honour at the head of the room and made comfortable on colourful cushions called *tushak* with a pillow (*bolesht*) placed behind to lean back on before being offered tea.

Countless visitors and house guests are shocked by the generosity and hospitality of their hosts. And tea clearly plays an important role in this tradition.

But after learning about tea in Afghanistan from Jawed and reading about the traditions of tea and hospitality, I still wondered why and how Afghanistan had become a country with such a rich tea culture. We typically think about India, China and the U.K. as being top tea countries, but the numbers hint to Afghanistan as having a rich tea culture as well. Not only is Afghanistan a large importer of tea, *The Telegraph* notes Afghanistan has the #11 country for consumption per capita.

After talking to Mrs. Raj about tea in India, its tea culture began to make more sense. India has historically been a producer of tea. When the British set up tea plantations in India to compete with the Chinese, India naturally became a huge consumer of tea. In fact, in the Assam region—in which the bulk of India's black tea is produced—70 percent of the output is consumed domestically. But in Afghanistan, tea plantations are not as prevalent. They exist, but Afghanistan has to import tea on a massive scale to keep up with consumption.

I wondered to what extent Afghanistan's love of tea could be connected to British influence, but it soon became clear that this tea culture exists despite a troubled and often violent relationship between the two countries. They fought three wars against each other! In addition, Afghanistan was something of a British protectorate. Finally, in 1919, an Afghan king declared independence from the quasi-British rule.

The relationship between the two countries is interesting to notes because many historians think that in the United States, we do not have a strong tea culture because we resent the British and having been a colony. In Afghanistan, almost the opposite happened!

Although the pervasiveness of tea culture in Afghanistan came as a shock to me, it may not be as surprising to others more familiar with the area. Based on conversations with Jawed, Afghan tea culture is intertwined with their hospitable attitudes. While Afghans are not so focused on how their tea is made or in finding cool new tea varieties like we are in the United States, their undying love for the tradition of tea is impressive. To me, it seems that tea is more than just a product for them. Tea is a way to express hospitality, a way to spend time with family, a way to celebrate, and a way of life.

* *

JAWED'S SAFFRON TEA

This chapter's recipe is for saffron tea. I'd never heard about saffron tea until talking to Jawed. Saffron is a pricey commodity, but if you really feel like going the extra mile, try some saffron tea.

Saffron tea can be made by simply adding 2 to 3 strands of saffron to hot water and letting it steep. Or you can add other ingredients. There are many recipes for saffron green tea or ginger saffron tea. You can even have saffron milk tea. The possibilities are endless with saffron.

CHAPTER 4

PINKIES UP

———

Americans in the Ritz's tea room stand out because they work so hard to keep their pinkies extended while holding their teacup. It makes you look pretentious.

—BRUCE RICHARDSON, A BRITISH TEA
HISTORIAN DURING AN NPR INTERVIEW

The year is 2014; it's January and you're surfing Instagram, utterly unaware of the meme awakening going on around you. In January of 2014, images of Kermit the Frog began to surface with the tag #kermitmemes. It wasn't until June of that same fateful year that Kermit the Frog became associated with the phrase "but that's none of my business." On June 20th, @thatsnoneofmybusiness on Instagram became responsible for the rise of our judgey friend. Since then, Kermit sipping tea has become a modern-day symbol of judgement calling.

Later, in 2015, when the Cleveland Cavaliers beat the Golden State Warriors in a highly contested playoff game, Lebron James of the Cavs wore a hat embroidered with Kermit the Frog, a nod to the already-legendary meme. Many experts doubted that James' star status would overcome the stacked Golden State Warriors line-up. However, James proved them wrong, making the naysayers seem silly. One commentator, James Plante, at "The Verge," wrote, "The hat made James' message clear: 'We just beat the best team in basketball. But that's none of my business.'"

But to me, the key part of this judgment-calling meme is that Kermit is found sipping tea. In the classic rendition pictured below, Kermit is sipping a golden brown cuppa Lipton tea. The image is simple, clear, and it looks like Kermit is living his best life. Kermit is calling judgment and Kermit is clearly correct about whatever shade he is throwing or whatever negative judgment he is passing.

It may seem somewhat random that Kermit is sipping tea, but even the phrase "sipping tea" has judgmental origins. Urban Dictionary defines "sipping tea" as, "to subtly yet effectively toss shade." Have you ever heard the phrase "spill the tea?" For ages, tea has been associated with gossiping.

These connotations of gossiping and judgement calling contribute to why many people associate tea with being pretentious.

When I think of tea as pretentious, I think of the British. After all, they invented afternoon tea with finger sandwiches, dainty cups, and "manners," right?

According to NPR, they did. As the legend goes, Anna Maria Russell, Duchess of Bedford, sparked the afternoon tea craze because of her hunger pains in between lunch and dinner.

Back in the 1830s, for the upper class, lunch was served at noon but dinner wasn't served any earlier than 7:30 p.m. As someone who enjoys a good snickety-snack, I relate with the Duchess of Bedford. How could she not get hungry before dinner?

To solve her hunger pains, she started ordering tea and snacks to her bedchamber. Eventually, her friends and the rest of the royal court started joining her. And when you're a duchess with company, you can't just sit in your PJs to enjoy your tea. You have to go all out.

As an NPR article notes, "Afternoon tea was hardly a humble affair then. Nor is it today." Back then you would find "crustless finger sandwiches and an array of dainty scones, cakes, macaroons and other tempting nibbles" accompanying your tea. It was also important to find your manners and "place your napkin on your lap and stir gently." NPR says, "Splashing tea, clinking cups and spoons and finger licking will make you appear beastly."

As we can see, afternoon tea in the British tradition is no casual affair.

This fancy tea time is what I was deathly afraid of when I first visited England. It was the summer after my high school graduation and I went to Europe with my friends Izzy, Lauren, Sofia, and our chaperone, Megan.

During this trip, we went to Spain, Italy, Ireland, and even Poland. But we also spent a week in Emsworth, England at Izzy's grandmother's house. Izzy's grandma is Gretta Pescod, but we all call her Ouma. Yes, that Ouma that you heard about in the introduction of this book.

She's the sweetest woman, but isn't afraid to speak the truth. Exactly what you'd imagine from an English grandma. Izzy has a "free bird" personality and now I know exactly where she got it.

*   *

It's been three years since I visited Ouma and I've forgotten what English tea is really like. Luckily, Ouma was willing to talk to me over a video call about English tea time.

She began by saying that "lots of British people like what we call 'builder's tea.' It's called that because it's strong tea. The worker men like strong tea." However, not all English tea needs to be this strong.

For example, Ouma said, "When you're taking tea in the afternoon, you might have green tea." It depends on people's tea preferences. That explains why Ouma served weaker black tea with lots of sugar to us while we were visiting! For most of us, it was our first English tea time and she wanted to make us Americans like tea, so she made sure to add lots of sugar.

I asked Ouma what types of food typically accompany a proper English tea time. "We eat cucumber sandwiches with all the crusts cut off. Very, very small cucumber sandwiches, with bread, butter, and cucumber. Then we also have tiny cakes. Not big, huge cakes. You could have sponge cakes, delicate little cakes." She made sure to note that this was only during a more formal tea time. She said that when we visited, we took tea with her, but it was more casual. She just gave us whatever sweets she had around.

Although Ouma prefers a more casual tea time, she did note that "you can go out to tea in restaurants these days and they have a lovely three-tiered tray. So you have sandwiches on the bottom tier, on the mid tier you have scones with jam and cream, and on the top tier you have your cakes."

Now, scones are also an important part of English tea time—they are a fan favorite. "The funny thing about scones is you can either say 'skon' or 'scone.' You cut the scones in half. Some people put cream and then jam, and other people like jam and then cream. I like jam and then cream. It's really nice to have Cornish cream." Cornish cream is a thick sort of butter that's deliciously fattening.

I wanted to know when the British typically have tea. From Mrs. Raj, we learned that in India, they take tea breaks during the day. But in Afghanistan, from Jawed's stories, tea is on tap all day! Ouma reports that the British typically take tea at particular times.

She says, "We drink tea for breakfast and coffee mid-morning, tea in the afternoon, and then coffee at night." I was shocked to hear that coffee was part of the daily routine at all. The British are so proud of their tea, you'd think it's all they drink.

Nonetheless, Ouma says, "People drink more coffee nowadays than they used to, but tea is more of a tradition that we always have."

I've always wondered at what age people start drinking tea. I really only started drinking coffee or tea (for the caffeine) junior and senior year of high school. But in a country like

England with a big tea culture, I wondered if most people start earlier. Ouma insisted that although they start early, "you obviously don't have tea when you're a baby. But you start probably from six or seven."

Overall, Ouma prescribed a pretty specific tea culture around English tea time. But she still asserted her preference for more casual tea times. "Now obviously when I invite people over I don't have cucumber sandwiches or fancy tiered plates or cakes. I serve whatever I have. At the moment, I have mince pies and I'm having people over for tea this Friday."

* *

Back when I visited England three years ago, I wasn't a huge tea fan and I didn't exactly have those proper British manners (plot twist: I still don't).

However, I had nothing to worry about. Our tea time with Ouma was nothing like I had imagined, in the best way. We didn't have dainty cups or crustless sandwiches, but instead enjoyed hearty cups of tea, amazing homemade sweets, a great view of the Emsworth bay, and good conversation.

During our first tea time that week, we were pretty jet-lagged. Ouma had to scream upstairs where we were napping, "WAKE

UP! WAKE UP! I don't hear movement! It's tea time!" It was only four o'clock, we still had a lot of time before dinner with her friends, but Ouma insisted we couldn't miss tea time.

We all slowly made it downstairs to her outdoor patio with a view of the bay. She poured piping hot glasses of tea into a mismatched set of mugs, making sure to pour the milk first, then the tea, and added heaps of sugar.

The cups were so hot! But that was okay—it helped combat the brisk ocean air. We started eating her sweets and Lauren and I began dipping them into the tea because it was still too hot to drink.

Lauren suddenly spoke up, "Oh! Wait, we probably aren't supposed to dip our sweets into the tea. That's probably not proper."

Ouma laughed and said, "It's not quite proper," in her British accent. But she assured us, "It's okay. We are just enjoying tea at home. We don't need to be proper to enjoy a proper British tea." My fears of messing up tea time suddenly vanished. Tea isn't so pretentious after all, even to the British.

*   *

Just like Ouma helped break the myth that all tea is pretentious, I hope this book will help you realize that tea is a beverage we can all enjoy in our own way.

Recently, I went to office hours for my branding class, taught by professor Debora Thompson, to ask questions regarding a class project. We got to talking and I told her about the book I am writing about tea and seeing tea in a new light. As an expert in branding, she started thinking about the brand that tea had as a commodity. Immediately, she noted that tea had this "pretentious" association. She brought up how she thought about "old, British tea times" and even modern day tea snobs who would never go near a tea bag.

She mentioned an NPR segment she heard one morning on her way to work that inspired her comments on the branding of tea. The talk was an interview of chef Julia Turshen on NPR's Fresh Air segment.

Turshen was promoting her new cookbook titled "Small Victories," which is all about simple, flexible recipes that anyone could use. While Turshen has helped many others author cookbooks, this is the first one where she is the main author.

Readers could say her book originated from laziness in the kitchen. Turshen recognizes this critique in the interview, but she also says because of this laziness standpoint, "every recipe is introduced with a small victory." The point of each recipe is that there is some part of the recipe that could be translated into new creations. Each recipe comes with a "tip or a technique that just makes cooking a little bit more approachable."

For example, one of Turshen's most popular small victories is her olive oil fried eggs. The recipe is, simply, to "fry them in olive oil and you serve them with yogurt." However, the trick to perfecting this small victory is "just to put a couple drops of water in the pan—and in the pan itself, not on the egg. And then cover the pan immediately. And what happens is that little tiny bit of water—like, not even a teaspoon, just a few drops off, you know, your fingertips—creates a little bit of steam. And the lid will trap the steam in there. So you almost create this little sort of stovetop, like, steam oven." This DIY steam oven unlocks the perfect fried egg. The beauty of this fried egg is that it's easy to make, is a good source of protein, and can be added to other ingredients and used in many kinds of meals.

According to Turshen, "The goal is just to empower home cooks." What good is a recipe for an at-home cook if they can't understand the directions? That was one of the key points for Turshen while writing the book. She says, "Sometimes I think of myself as kind of, like, a home cooking translator of, like, how can I translate this material so someone can do it successfully at home?"

Professor Thompson's takeaway from the NPR segment was that Turshen was working to make something accessible to a larger market. As a professor of branding, you could see her analytical mind thinking about "Small Victories" as a way to reposition home cooking so it becomes appealing to people who lack a technical background in cooking.

What if we looked at tea in the same way? I've always hated how pretentious tea can be and after researching and interviewing experts in tea, I've come to realize that a certain amount of snobbiness is part of the tea industry. When I started researching this book and interviewing professionals in the industry, I was almost scared away from the topic altogether. I realized I had no idea about half the vocabulary they were using. I was only an expert in my own experiences with tea.

Have you ever been to a fancy restaurant, tried to order off the wine list, and felt so out of your league? Well, I've had many similar experiences at tea shops. You walk into the store and make too much noise tripping over their oriental rugs. Then you stumble over to the menu boards and squint, trying to make out the simplest cup of green tea only to find there are like 30 different types. Next, you have to decide what price range you're going for. You don't want to buy the cheapest one, but you also don't want to spend $15 on a cuppa tea. So you go with the $8 one hoping the server doesn't hate you for being an uncultured swine. Once you finally get your tea, you wander over to find a nook to dive into your book or work and start feeling at home. It's honestly so stressful I work up a sweat every time.

After sitting in a few more tea shops for this book and talking to several owners and learning a bit more about their shops, I've become more comfortable. In fact, the people working at the tea shops are usually helpful for finding your perfect drink for the day. You just have to ask!

One of my favorite tea shops in Washington, D.C., is called Calabash. The first time I visited was a Friday afternoon. I'd had a tough week and was feeling fatigued. I was intrigued to see that their menu is organized by the herbal benefits of their drinks. There's a whole section for love potions. The server asked me what kind of drink I needed and I thought for a second. I decided to open up and said, "Something under the love life category, what's your favorite?" The server chuckled a little and suggested a tea that suited me very well.

Going back to the idea behind the "Small Victories" cook-book, tea doesn't need to be difficult and pretentious. Yes, it's 100 percent important for the world to have tea experts and people who actually know what they are talking about to preserve cultural traditions of tea and to maintain knowl-edge on the benefits of all the different varieties. For example, the server at Calabash used his knowledge of the complexity of tea to help me narrow down the choices. Although this complexity exists, it shouldn't prevent the simpletons of the world (like me) from enjoying a cuppa tea.

So to help more people enjoy the goodness of tea, I want to break down some of the barriers to enjoying it. Like professor Thompson taught us in class, key associations affect how brands are viewed and consumed in the world. In the case of tea, I don't want the association of being pretentious to distract anyone from enjoying this great beverage.

The last thing this book needs to be is another pretentious piece of work about tea. Although I do want to help beginners break into the world of tea, I also want to help everyone, beginners to experts, connect back to the experience part of tea and realizing it can be so much more than just the tea leaves.

* *

OUMA'S ENGLISH TEA

To accompany your reading, Ouma has given us her personal English tea recipe.

Ouma gave us a recipe for English black tea. Although English tea can be served with any tea of your choosing, Ouma always uses the PG Tips brand of black tea. It's cheap and simple, yet delicious. It does the trick!

While steeping PG Tips black tea does not require extreme precision, if you are enjoying a nicer black tea, perhaps in loose leaf form, you will want to make sure to boil it at around 200 degrees Fahrenheit.

Luckily, Ouma's English tea time doesn't require this precision.

"If I was having friends to tea, I'd make a pot of tea and put some tea bags in it. I would heat the pot beforehand, which is very important, and then put two or three tea bags in once the water boils." Ouma noted the importance of bringing the water to a boil before adding the tea bags.

Ouma also says to use two *or* three tea bags because "it depends on how people like their tea, but whether they like it weaker or stronger."

"I always add the milk first in the cup beaker or mug, but some people add it after they pour the tea." That the milk is added first is very important to Ouma and everyone in her family. "You always need to put your milk in first. If you ask a chemist, there is a different reaction between the milk and the tea."

To finish off your English tea time, Ouma says to "add sugar to taste and serve with sweet biscuits, cookies, chocolates, or cucumber sandwiches!"

CHAPTER 5

TASTING QUALITY

———

It's a placebo effect. There's no way it really tasted that different.

—MR. MA ON EXPENSIVE JASMINE TEAS

Mr. Ma was born and raised in Taiwan before leaving home to go to school in the United States. Mr. Ma is one of my good friend's parents, who also happens to like tea.

Mr. Ma often travels to China for business. And on one of these trips, he went right before his wife's birthday. He wanted to bring her back something special. In China, lots of people gift tea because it's considered safe. Mr. Ma said, "Tea doesn't really offend anyone who is Chinese."

But for Mr. Ma, jasmine tea was something special for his wife: It is her favorite tea.

So, Mr. Ma decided to go to the most famous tea shop on Wangfujing Street in Beijing. Wangfujing is a famous street that has been popular for shopping ever since the Ming dynasty.

The tea shop had thousands of teas and Mr. Ma was overwhelmed. He went up to the shopkeeper and said, "I want to taste some jasmine teas for my wife."

The shop keeper asked, "What kind?"

But Mr. Ma did not know what type of jasmine tea. He wanted to get his wife something of very high quality, but didn't want to break his bank on tea leaves.

Mr. Ma told me that at this tea shop "they weigh their tea leaves in ounces. And they can range from 20 RMD to 1,000 RMD per ounce." That's anywhere from $3 to $150 per ounce!

Not knowing which type of jasmine tea he wanted to buy, Mr. Ma asked the shop keeper, "What's the difference between the jasmine teas?"

The shop keeper replied, "They are all different qualities and you can tell by the smell." She proceeded to open a few jasmine tea jars for Mr. Ma to smell.

He couldn't tell the difference. So he asked, "Can I smell your most expensive jasmine tea?"

The shopkeeper said, "Unfortunately, we are out of stock." Mr. Ma was unsatisfied with their response. He theorized they weren't letting him smell the most expensive kind because there was really no difference.

Mr. Ma decided to settle on purchasing a few mid—to upper-range jasmine teas so that when he went home and gave them to his wife, they could test the teas and compare them. He told me that he thought, "It's like a placebo effect. There's no way it really tastes that different."

But after gifting the jasmine teas and trying them out, Mr. Ma admitted that he could tell a little difference when it came to trying the most expensive of the teas. "It tasted a little better. But I don't know if it was worth the price difference."

Ultimately, Mr. Ma didn't know how to trust his sense of smell to determine quality in the tea shop. The only way he could really tell was by tasting the teas after he bought them.

*   *

Like Mr. Ma, a barrier for me to enjoying tea was my lack of skill at assessing its quality. When you're in a fancy tea shop, it's easy to feel like you're being conned into buying expensive tea without any evidence that the price is justified. Only after traveling around a bit and doing more research for this book was I able to begin to understand the difference between good and bad tea.

I was scrolling through my Facebook feed the other day when a video about chocolate caught my eye. I've always been a chocoholic, so naturally, I had to watch.

This Facebook video was a *Business Insider* video featuring Angus Kennedy. Mr. Kennedy is a famous chocolate connoisseur who has his own magazine for the chocolate industry.

During this video, Mr. Kennedy explained the difference between high-quality and low-quality chocolate. He noted that one had a higher cocoa butter content, making it taste better. In addition, this bar contained more cocoa at around 70 percent. One of the easiest ways to tell if the bar is of high quality, according to Mr. Kennedy, is the sound it makes when you break off a piece of chocolate.

This higher the cocoa butter content, the more crisp the sound is when you break off a piece of chocolate. It should sound like a "click." This is because the chocolate has fewer sugary additives, less vegetable butter, and is more pure, which allows the chocolate to set harder.

The nicer chocolate should also have more of a fruity flavor without the bitterness. Cocoa beans taste bitter when they are roasted too long. Many people mistakenly think that all cocoa beans have a bitter flavor because many of us are used to the taste of low-quality chocolate.

This "click" test is one simple way to tell if you are consuming quality chocolate regardless of whether or not you have tasted that level of chocolate before. You don't have to know much about cocoa butter content, purity, or how the beans were roasted to know if the chocolate is quality or not.

After watching this video, I wondered how the typical, nonexpert tea drinker would know what good tea tastes like. Even after touring a tea plantation and doing all of the research for this book, I still questioned if I really knew what good tea tasted like or what made tea taste good.

I soon found that there are many complexities to consider when grading or determining tea quality and there are many organizations and laws that govern these determinations. The United Planters' Association of Southern India Tea Research Association lists all sorts of chemical compounds that must be present and at what levels to determine a tea's quality. The foundation also specifies the certain type of tea plant species—*Camellia sinensis*—to be considered tea.

The common person trying to enjoy tea probably doesn't have the time nor desire to get bogged down in all these details. However, in doing my research and drawing on my personal experiences, I have found that there are three main things to look out for in a good tea:

- lack of bitterness
- tea leaf size
- tea color

Like high-cocoa content chocolate bars, many people think quality teas are inherently bitter. This is not the case at all. Only low-quality or poorly brewed teas have bitter tastes.

*   *

One way to determine if a tea is of poor quality is the consistency of the size of its leaves. Oftentimes, different parts of the tea plant are used in tea blends as fillers. The best part of the tea plant are the freshest leaves near the top, which are harvested during the spring time of year. Lesser quality tea bags may use tea leaves harvested during nonpeak times or lower level leaves in their blends. They may use a few high-quality leaves, but fill up the rest of the tea bag or tea container with a leaf of a different quality.

One of the easiest ways to spot these lesser quality, filler leaves is by their size. Oftentimes, if you purchase a tea blend and can see a visible difference in tea leaf sizes (excluding cases where the blend is meant to include different leaves, for example, an herbal blend), it means one of the tea leaves is a cheap filler. Using fillers lowers the quality of the tea, may increase bitterness, and may decrease the number of times you can reuse the leaves.

There are many other ways to determine the quality of tea like taste or color, but those require brewing the tea beforehand. In Mr. Ma's story, we learned that smell is another way, but it can be difficult for the untrained nose to tell the difference. I've found that the consistency in tea leaf size is one of the best ways to tell if a tea is of low quality while you are in a tea store without the ability to sample.

Being able to make informed decisions about the quality of your tea is important because it affects how your tea tastes. I know this because I've experienced it firsthand.

*   *

All my life, I had been brewing tea by leaving a tea bag in a mug. I'd place the tea bag in the cup and pour water over, then enjoy. The tea bag stayed in the cup the entire time. I didn't realize how problematic this was until I visited China after my freshman year of college.

My family and I traveled for two weeks around China, from Beijing to Shanghai to Hangzhou. Then I went to Hong Kong, where I stayed to study abroad for four weeks.

During our trek through China, so many things about us stood out, including my very white and tall family. My curly blond hair got a lot of attention, while my 6' 2" mom and 6' 3" brother were equally interesting.

China was a whole new world. The experience was unreal. Big cities, big shopping malls, amazing tourism services, and ancient palaces all blew my mind.

But another underrated discovery for me was tea. We visited several tea shops during our time in China, but it was touring the tea plantation in Hangzhou that truly changed the way I saw tea.

Prior to tasting Hangzhou's famous green tea, I had always added sugar, milk, or honey to my tea. I brewed tea for so long without removing the tea bag that it became bitter. Adding sweetener was an imperative.

I remember trying sips of tea when I was a child and being disgusted by the bitterness. Even when I had afternoon tea in England, I had to dump sugar and cream into my black tea to erase some of the bitterness.

But after I tried green tea in China, brewed by a tea master during tea ceremonies, my perspective totally changed. This green tea was almost sweet. It wasn't flavorless, it was just less potent.

At the Hangzhou tea plantation, our guide was a middle-aged Chinese mother. She showed us around the grounds. It was a beautiful, hot, humid day and the fields were gorgeous. But I was happy when she took us indoors to their tea tasting room were it was cooler.

During the tea tasting, she showed us how to properly brew their green tea. "Place a tablespoon of the leaves into your tea pot and do a rinse," she explained. First you must rinse the tea leaves in hot water to release some of the bitter flavors and clean the leaves. I had almost always used tea bags up to that point in my life, so I had no idea you had to "rinse" tea leaves before actually using them.

Next, she said, "Let the tea leaves infuse for two minutes. The longer you let the tea leaves sit, the more strong the tea gets. If you don't like bitter tea, just shorten your infusing time."

Brilliant. Why had I never thought of that? It felt like my whole life had been a lie up to that point. I was leaving my tea bags in my tea, living life like an idiot always having to add sweetener to combat the bitterness.

When it finally came time to taste the green tea, my mind was blown. It was so sweet. How could this be? All my life, green tea had been bitter, but then I hop on a plane to China and all of a sudden it's sweet. I know China is literally on the other half of the globe, but the difference in the taste of green tea was wild.

A big part of the difference in taste is due to brewing time. If you let the tea leaves sit for too long or at the wrong temperature, the flavoring becomes totally different.

In general, with most teas, the shorter you steep, the less potent the tea is and, in general, less bitter. However, if you are following the instructions on your tea and still get an aggressively bitter taste, your tea may not be of as high quality as you originally thought.

However, another problem that led to bitterness in my tea was that I had only ever used cheap tea bags. Before Hangzhou, I had never experienced loose leaf tea.

But after this plantation tour, I realized how important tea quality is to taste. It really does matter. When I asked the tour guide what made this tea so much better quality than tea in the United States, she said it had to do with what part of the tea leaf they used. "Many tea importers in the United States try to get the cheapest tea possible," she explained. "They buy the tea not during the peak season or the cheaper parts of the tea leaf, making it not taste as good as the tea we sell here."

It was a brilliant sales plug, but she does have a legitimate point. U.S. tea importers can blend different parts of the tea leaf together, using the cheaper parts as filler in their tea bags. They can also buy tea off season, using the cheaper leaves. These decisions will impact the quality of their product.

However, not all tea manufacturers in the United States do this. In later chapters, I will highlight companies that source the best tea leaves and don't cut corners.

This tea tour opened my eyes to how important the quality of tea can be to a person's tea experience. While tea of lesser quality and more economical pricing certainly has a place in the U.S. market, most people simply do not understand what they are or are not paying for. I certainly didn't.

*   *

An emerging innovation in tea is using it as an ingredient in cocktails. The cocktail industry has experienced an awakening in craft cocktails, a sort of Renaissance. One of the bartenders at the forefront of this awakening is Jim Meehan.

Meehan has created concoctions at a variety of fine restaurants; he even helped the infamous PDT bar in New York City rise to the legend it's known as today. Meehan has also been able to add a few books to his resume. He's the author of *The PDT Cocktail Book* and *Meehan's Bartender's Manual*, which detail some of the famous cocktails he helped create at PDT and a guide for bar operations as well as the history of cocktails, respectively.

It's fair to say Meehan is a guru and knows what he's talking about when it comes to a good cocktail. After checking out all of his accomplishments in his industry, I'd be nervous to go get drinks with him. I'd make a fool of myself!

However, Meehan understands the importance of serving his audience. He didn't always create fantastic cocktails. In fact, he got his start at a crappy college bar called State Street Brats. In an interview, he said he has "made every single crazy shot you could ever imagine—Snake Bites, B52s, shots of Jaeger." That's right, the same man that created the refined Green Tea Punch—a mixture of sencha green tea, mint tea, and rum— was also responsible for the sugar-induced hangovers of barely legal college students.

When an interviewer at FirstWeFeast.com confronted him about this past he said, "Cocktails are very much like fashion. It would be easy for me to look down at those drinks and say,

'I'm so above that, it's disgusting.' But the drink resonated in that audience."

Meehan's quote speaks to how I think we should view tea. Having high-quality, expensive tea is nice. But sometimes it just doesn't resonate with the audience. Sometimes I enjoy a $15 cup of quality tea, but I also like drinking my PG Tips with milk and sugar. It may not be perfectly smooth or naturally sweet, but it reminds me of the time I spent in England taking tea with Ouma and my friends.

In fact, Meehan cherishes the time he spent at State Street Brats to the point of even including it in an article that calls out specific drinks that made his career. Another drink that made the article? Milwaukee's Best beer. Meehan understands his cocktail career is more than being pretentious about the ingredients. He included Milwaukee's Best because it was the first drink he ever had. And yes, it was at a horrible high school party and he got sick because of it, but it was an important launching point in his career. The drink had emotional and sentimental importance.

For me, likewise, tea has a sentimental importance that extends beyond quality considerations. There are many functional benefits to drinking tea, and I have enjoyed learning about tea rituals from different countries, but tea also serves as a conduit to good memories. Some of the most valuable advice I have received and the most beneficial bitch sessions of mine have happened over a cup of tea.

Hearing Meehan's story and realizing those lackluster drinks had a purpose in his career got me thinking about how certain teas resonate with different people.

For example, I came across an article from *The Onion*—a satirical news site—about a local man trying to relax with tea. The article poked fun at an overly stressed man really wanting the relaxing tea to "live up to its lofty promises." A quote from the fake news article reads, "Local man Pete McCartin, 29, told reporters Thursday that a fresh-brewed mug of purportedly relaxation-promoting tea had better fucking work." McCartin didn't care about the quality of his tea. He just cared that it "had better fucking work" to relax him and make him "placid as hell." McCartin is a simple man just trying to harness the power of tea in his everyday life. It's satire, but it's relatable, isn't it?

While the most trained tea sommeliers can easily determine the quality of a tea with great accuracy, being able to identify tea quality isn't everything. People use different types of tea in different types of situations. Quality is only the beginning of the story. Of course, tea quality is important if you are looking for something special or unique like Mr. Ma was, because you don't want to be ripped off. However, in everyday situations, quality can be a secondary consideration to how you think the tea tastes.

Some people like strong tea. Some people like softer tea. Ultimately, the tea you drink should be something you can enjoy. Like Meehan says, it's important to make sure the tea "resonates" with you. For me, sometimes that means enjoying a cup of PG Tips. PG Tips might not be the most expensive or highest quality tea, but it's the type of tea Ouma takes during British tea time and it brings back great memories for me. I love it!

Other times, I may want a high quality tea. It depends on my mood and what experience I want. Maybe I want to sit in an expensive tea shop with a friend to taste new flavors or learn more about the world's different types of tea. Even when I go to a nice tea shop to search out a quality tea, I place more importance on the experience of being in the tea shop, learning about the new tea, and even the relaxing elements of the tea shop.

The lesson here is that although knowing your tea quality is important, it should not be everything. Our tea experiences can not be limited to obsessing over quality or we will lose out on all the other cool experiences that come with drinking a cup of tea.

* *

HANNAH'S FAVORITE GREEN TEA

Up until my tea adventure in China, I had thought that green tea was always bitter. Once my eyes were opened to the natural sweetness of Chinese green tea, I only drank the tea we had purchased while there. But eventually, I ran out and needed to find a new green tea. Enter Rishi Tea.

At the time, my parents were traveling in California and they were staying at a fancy hotel. I think the occasion was their anniversary and they went to a health and wellness retreat type of hotel. Classic California.

At this hotel, each room had a well-stocked wet bar plus coffee and tea. My mom loved the tea in their hotel room so much that she shipped me some of the tea sachets that she "gathered" from the hotel in a care package to Georgetown. Crafty, mom.

These tea sachets were made by Rishi Tea. She sent me a black mango blend, chamomile, and a few classic green teas. Each tea sachet had such bold flavor, I was shocked it was coming from a tea bag. Although the black mango and chamomile were good, I'm a die-hard green tea fan and Rishi's green tea sachets were out of this world!

The way my mom and I discovered Rishi Tea was no accident. Rishi is a relatively new company based in Milwaukee. With more limited distribution and advertising, one of their strategies has been to place their products in luxury hotels. In Chapter 7, we will hear from a Rishi Tea representative about this strategy and more about their brand's amazing story.

Almost instantly, Rishi Tea's Jade Cloud Green Tea sachets became my favorite tea of all time. As a result, I always have a Jade Cloud sachet in my backpack at school, just in case I feel like a good cup of tea.

Rishi Tea's distribution is limited in terms of retail outlets. However, the company has an extensive website where it sells all types of tea, both loose leaf varieties and its amazing sachets. You can also find certain Rishi Tea blends on Amazon Prime!

For its Jade Cloud tea sachets, Rishi recommends steeping for two to three minutes at 180 degrees Fahrenheit. As I often drink these tea sachets on the go, I don't pay much attention to the temperature. In terms of steeping time, go shorter if you don't want as aggressive of a flavor and go longer for a bolder tea. Rishi's tea sachets pack a punch, so I often go shorter—around one minute—and I often reuse the tea bags once or twice. The more I reuse the tea leaves though, the longer I steep. It's also important to remember that the caffeine content also decreases with each use.

CHAPTER 6

TEA IN THE UNITED STATES

———

Young people created subcultures and allegiance to their generation. They began rejecting the old—which in Britain, this was tea.

—ERIKA RAPPAPORT, BRITISH CONSUMERISM HISTORIAN

The year was 1773. It was December, but the British colonists in America could hardly get into the Christmas spirit. Although happy to be living in America, a land of opportunity, the British crown was frankly pissing the colonists off. Yet another tax was being imposed on these free people. And a tax is enough to get mad about, but a tax without representation in the royal courts...

How. Dare. They.

The American colonists had enough. Their blood was boiling. It was time to be bolder than a cup of strong black tea.

On the night of December 16, 1773, a group of colonists disguised as American Indians stormed the Boston Harbor, where three ships full of British tea from India were waiting to be unloaded. And boy oh boy were the colonists going to help the British unload their tea—right into the Boston Harbor.

Earlier that year, the British had passed the Tea Act of 1773. This act not only taxed everyone's beloved tea, but it required that American colonists buy British tea from India. Though cheaper than other tea (because of its lesser quality, might I add), the requirement to buy British tea limited colonists' freedom of choice and imposed yet another tax without representation.

Contrary to popular belief, the Boston Tea Party was not a riot, according to Joanne Freeman from Yale University. "They wanted to make a point about tea to the British," she notes. See, the colonists did not care about damaging the ships or harbor itself. That was not the point. The colonists were specifically mad about the tea tax and only sought to destroy the tea.

The Boston Tea Party will go down as one of the greatest tea parties ever. Many people see this as a symbol of American rebellion against not only the tax, but against British ideals. If the British own the cup of tea, what better way to reject their imperialistic ways than by throwing that cup of tea into the ocean that divides us?

*   *

I knew this idea of Americans rejecting the British cup of tea would be worth exploring after I talked to a peer in one of my classes. We were doing an in-class activity where we had to write down all the things we liked or considered hobbies. Tea came up in several of my answers and this classmate noticed.

"You mention tea a lot. That's kind of weird because like tea isn't really a thing in the U.S.," he said.

Interesting. I'd never thought about that. We talked a little bit about it and he said, "Maybe it's because of the Boston Tea Party. Now we just hate tea because we resented everything British at that time."

My fellow student brought up a good point, and I decided to further explore this theory. I sought out Erika Rappaport, a consumer-focused historian at University of California at Santa Barbara, who had published a book on tea and the British empire called, A Thirst for Empire: How Tea Shaped the Modern World.

My main question for her was "Why is tea not a thing in the United States? Is it because of the Boston Tea Party?" The answer I got was far more complex than I expected. I got to chat with her personally when she came to the University of Richmond to make a presentation and promote her book. What followed placed my simple question in a larger context and perhaps raised more questions than answers.

*   *

During Rappaport's presentation, one of the PowerPoint slides was an image of a "Keep Calm and Carry On" poster, except it was parodied to read "Keep Calm and Drink Tea" with a British flag behind it.

We all know the British love their tea and we often credit them with the creation and development of tea globally. After all, their great empire was fueled by tea's production and consumption. However, tea was stolen by Europeans from the Chinese during the 17th century exploration period.

Portuguese missionaries first brought tea back to Europe and it was later commercialized by the Dutch. But it was the Scottish businessmen who pushed the taste for tea to a wider market, especially among the British.

Tea was first introduced to the British by Catherine of

Braganza, a Portuguese royal. Catherine married England's King Charles II in 1662 to become the Queen of England. In 1662, she made the trip from Portugal to England to begin her new life as queen. And with her, she brought crates labeled "Transporte de Ervas Aromatics" full of loose leaf tea. This label created the acronym "T.E.A," thus, the British coined the name "tea" for the loose leaves.

Queen Catherine simply brought tea, which was quite common among Portuguese nobility, to England. What made tea very popular in England was the Duchess of Bedford's desire for an afternoon snack at royal court in 1837. The Duchess of Bedford is credited with making "afternoon tea" a British institution.

Before the mid-1880s, tea was reserved for the upper echelons of European society. Tea was an expensive import. The British taxed tea at incredibly high rates. It wasn't until this tax fell and Scottish businessmen bought plantations themselves in British colonies that tea became more affordable.

After tea became popular as an afternoon experience in England among the upper class, Scottish and British businessmen ventured to India and even parts of East Africa to establish their own tea plantations instead of importing tea from China. During the mid-1800s, these Scottish and British families controlled all parts of the tea supply chain. For example, the uncle would own the plantation while the cousin did advertising in Britain and the father owned the retail outlets.

By the 1930s, British businesses controlled two-thirds of the tea produced and consumed globally. They also controlled other ancillary businesses like boxing companies, machine producers, and other packaging.

The industry was able to accomplish this monopoly through tea trade associations. There were several tea associations in Asia. However, there were two notable tea associations in India, one in each tea producing region of India. One was based in Calcutta (and later London) and was called the Indian Tea Association. The other was based in Ceylon and called the Planters Association of Ceylon (now evolved into TEA—Tea Exporter's Association).

The Indian Tea Association was formed in 1881 to "to promote orderly growth and collective thinking in Tea," according to its website. The Indian Tea Association is geographically associated with Calcutta and Assam Tea. Botanist Robert Bruce is responsible for discovering a variation of tea plant, local to India (which natives had been using for years). It is this tea plant that is responsible for what we know as Assam black tea today. In 1823, Calcutta shipped out its first crate of Assam black tea to England. From Calcutta and the Assam region, tea began to grow in India, thanks to the native tea plant.

The Planters Association of Ceylon was established in 1854, after tea was brought to Ceylon. In 1824, botanists in Ceylon had experimented with Chinese tea plants but failed. Later, in 1839, tea plant seeds from Calcutta were sent to Ceylon. It was these tea plant seeds from Calcutta that were used to grow the tea industry in Ceylon.

Often credited as the father of the tea industry in Ceylon, the Scotsman James Taylor opened the first tea plantation in Ceylon in 1867. In 1873, the first tea shipment of Ceylon tea from Taylor's plantation arrived in England.

At this time, coffee plantations were very popular in India. But, when the "coffee tea leaf disease" struck in 1870, coffee plantations lost all their harvest and began converting to tea plantations. By the 1880s, almost all coffee plantations had converted to tea plantations to survive. The Planters Association of Ceylon continued to help grow tea in Ceylon and establish Ceylon tea as a tea brand that represented great quality. Once Ceylon changed their name to Sri Lanka, tea associations in the area evolved. Now, the main tea association is know as T.E.A., or the Tea Exporter's Association and aims to protect Sri Lanka's status as a tea country of the world.

These tea associations were revolutionary. They were truly global and encompassed all players in the tea value chain. From tea plantation owners to exporters, advertisers, and shop owners in England, each part of the value chain was committed to boosting tea sales as a commodity. What Rappaport found most interesting in her research was that these associations invented a tax on themselves to support general advertising for tea as a commodity. At the time, association taxes like these were relatively unheard of. This tax was based on the value of tea exported from the region. People in the tea business thought that promoting tea was essential to selling the product and were willing to contribute to this tax.

At the St. Louis World Fair in 1904, tea associations poured lots of money into their exhibits. British tea exporters were eager to get a piece of the U.S. tea market. The British had expanded their love of tea to their other colonies, like India and parts of Africa, by using them for production of tea. Even though the United States was no longer one of their colonies, the British saw the United States as a new market with exponential growth opportunities in the sale of tea.

*   *

So, more than a century after the Boston Tea Party, the British were still trying to expand their tea empire to consumers in the United States. But despite pouring all this money into world fairs and subsequent advertising, tea hasn't really stuck here the way it has in other cultures.

Why is this? Rappaport argues that it goes deeper than the Boston Tea Party. While the tea party and its representation of resentment toward British colonialism may answer some of our questions, it's not the whole picture. It wasn't so much that colonists hated the British taxes; it actually has more to do social changes taking place after World War II.

Back in the 1930s, tea was still a hit in the British empire. The industry was thriving! However, during World War II, and for several years after, when goods were being rationed, the tea industry feared that tea's popularity would decline if it was hard to get and people learned to live without it. Big business went to great lengths to make sure the people still had a little tea because they didn't want consumers to "lose their taste for tea," Rappaport said.

In fact, Ouma does not remember tea being rationed during the war. While I was talking with Ouma about tea, she began speaking about the war because I asked her if she always takes her tea with sugar.

She said that while "most people nowadays probably don't drink it with sugar, when I was a child, my brother and I gave up sugar during the war, so that my father, who was working—obviously—could eat sugar. We were on rations, so he needed to have the sugar in his tea."

When I asked Ouma if she remembered the tea itself being rationed, she said, "You know, I don't remember that. . . . Tea would have come from Ceylon then. But, I'm not sure. I was only 13 or 14, so I wouldn't have been a heavy tea drinker then. I don't remember about tea rationing."

Rappaport believes consumers can lose their taste for commodities and in the 1960s, British people were turning away from tea.

With the 1960s came a feeling of rebellion among American and British youth. In the United States, young people were rebelling against wars. Similar social changes were happening in Britain. Tea was a casualty of this new youth culture.

Despite the tea industry's great efforts to make sure the British "didn't lose their taste for tea," consumer behavior shifted after the war. Rappaport reports, "Young people created subcultures and allegiance to their generation. They began rejecting the old—which in Britain, this was tea."

In the United States, we didn't really have a "taste for tea" to begin with. But in countries like Britain, tea and its traditional connotations did not fit with this post-war vibe of rebellion. But what did fit with the rebellious youth culture of the 1960s in Britain? Coffee.

That's right. Even in Britain, coffee shops began popping up. Rappaport says, "After the war, immigrants brought the tradition of coffeehouses to Britain." Coffeehouses were the cool place to be. Coffee shops embraced the nature of rock 'n' roll. They were a place were you could get served a Coke and soak up all things rebellious. They even put out American vibes and British youngsters liked this. Tea just couldn't keep up.

Rappaport explains that "coffee bars got an association of modernity," while tea was seen as a thing of the past. In contrast, coffee was considered "exotic and part of night life and dating culture."

So how did big tea business react to this change in consumer behavior? Well, first, they resented American culture and the coffeehouses made popular by immigrants. But, they also realized how deeply tea was rooted in British imperialism and how unpopular this was among the younger public.

The British tea industry began pouring money into marketing schemes to break tea's associations with older times and pretentious rituals. A big part of this scheme was a campaign called "Join the tea set," created by an ad agency for the UK Tea Council.

Back in the day, a "set" was a popular group of people, like the "in crowd" or the cool clique at school. The UK Tea Council's "tea set" campaign was cringeworthy: They had tea endorsed by sad, B-list British celebrities and made punny buttons and "tea" shirts. They even put on a rock 'n' roll concert sponsored by tea. Needless to say, the campaign didn't work.

The UK Tea Council tried so hard, but only came off as "appropriating young left culture," according to Rappaport. Previous associations of tea with British culture, imperialism, and fancy afternoon rituals were so strong that the UK Tea Council could not pivot the brand image. The UK Tea Council ultimately failed to change the brand image of tea to fit in with the young, hip, rebellious tone of the time. With all these issues of brand image in their home country, it's no wonder that had trouble solidifying the British version of tea in the United States.

*   *

This British example may shed light on why tea never caught on in the United States. It's not that we consciously hate tea because we declared independence from Britain. Many other countries have a thriving tea culture despite declaring independence from Britain (Afghanistan, for example). As Americans, we never identified with the formal tradition of serving tea. Maybe tea time just didn't fit with our American ideals of equality or independence.

However, this exploration of U.S. history and British history in the context of tea doesn't mean that tea businesses don't do well in the United States. After all, down South we have an obsession with "sweet tea:" iced tea with an abundance of sweetness. As this new third wave of tea takes hold in the United States, we have big tea companies, like Teavana and Tazo (under the umbrella of Starbucks and Unilever, respectively) along with niche companies, redefining what tea means for Americans.

*   *

One great example of a tea company that is taking a fresh approach to the U.S. market is Rishi Tea—yep, the same Rishi Tea that my mom "gathered" from the hotel to send back to me. Joshua Kaiser founded Rishi Tea in 1997 after traveling to Asia and returning to the United States and not finding an adequate selection of traditional, hand crafted, loose leaf teas. Similar to single origin coffee beans and specialty wines, Kaiser believed there would be a market for high quality loose leaf tea if he brought it to the United States. So, Kaiser asked his longtime friend Benjamin Harrison to help him. They began hand-crafting specialty blends and hand-packaging Rishi Tea. They source their teas responsibly and work closely with producers to ensure each tea blend is certified organic.

Rishi Tea has grown to be one of the largest providers of specialty teas in the United States and continues to expand its reach. Jessica Conley, national director of hospitality at Rishi Tea, said, "Joshua's vision for Rishi Tea is exciting and has massive growth potential." In fact, one of the reasons she joined Rishi Tea in 2014 was because of Kaiser's excitement for the company. It was a big career move for Conley, who had previously worked in hospitality at a large food wholesaler, but Conley was excited to work for Kaiser and Rishi Tea was excited to have her talents.

Although Rishi Tea was founded on principles of selling more traditional, high quality tea, Kaiser and the team do not shy away from innovation. Realizing the sale of exclusively loose leaf tea limited their market potential, Kaiser wanted to expand into tea sachets (or tea bags) to reach more consumers. However, Kaiser did not settle for cheap paper tea bags that ruin the blend's purity and flavor. Instead, Kaiser invented special sachets. Conley noted, "Joshua refused to do with paper because it seeps into the tea or with cotton because cotton is one of the dirtiest products in the world. Nylon is petroleum based, but we are all organic and sustainable. Everything is to the degree of science."

Instead of using more traditional materials for Rishi's tea sachets, Kaiser used a vegetable product "made of tapioca and cornstarch," said Conley. She also noted that Rishi has "no glue on our sachet. The sachet is held together by heat sonic waves. When you're drinking Rishi Tea, you literally have no additional product in your cup besides the tea. It's biodegrad-able and does not leach anything into your cup."

These innovations in sachet material allow Rishi Tea to be served in convenient sachets without impairing the flavors in the tea. "Our sachets are very unique. Joshua wanted a loose leaf experience, but we have to cater to the people to drink tea in any opportunity." Conley continued, "we want to make it easy for people to consume tea, but we want to do it in a way that stresses the importance of great quality."

Conley noted that these innovations were critical to seeing Rishi Tea grow. The introduction of tea sachets has been essen-tial to Rishi's expansion into hotels. For example, you can find Rishi's tea sachets in many Four Seasons hotel rooms.

With a background in hospitality, Conley saw a huge oppor-tunity in serving Rishi Tea at luxury hotels. However, Rishi Tea did not break into the segment seamlessly. Conley and her team at Rishi Tea needed to carefully think about the customer needs, user experience, and brand touch points for the new segment.

Conley noted, "When we had to think about hospitality, the biggest struggle that I had with my owner is he is a tea purist. So, he wants everyone to be doing loose leaf tea because that's the proper way to do it." Conley and her team had to work on their strategy and what tea philosophy this new hospitality line would embrace. "In hospitality, there are so many people and workers that loose leaf tea is a very difficult strategy," said Conley.

Aside from looking at tea philosophies concerning loose leaf versus tea sachets, Conley and her team also had to consider a host of other questions. Who would be drinking the tea? How would they train hotel employees to serve the tea? What types of flavor profiles should they select?

Conley and her team paid close attention to all these details and many more to ultimately have a successful product launch. Conley shared, "It's a big world and there's a lot of opportunity for tea in the hospitality segment. Joining the team, developing a whole new product line, working with Joshua to source the products, and collecting competitor data played into the success of this line. We've had such great success. The company has gotten bigger because of this launch."

Rishi's innovation in tea sachets and subsequent expansion into the hospitality segment are just a few ways the company is working toward spreading Joshua's love for good tea to the broader U.S. consumer market. Rishi Tea also stays up-to-date on the latest innovations, like serving tea on tap. At the beginning of 2017, Rishi introduced tea taps in many tea and coffee shops in its hometown of Milwaukee, Wisconsin. These teas on tap have been best described by OnMilwaukee.com as a "new sparkling tea...(that) might just make you consider kicking your soda habit to the curb."

Rishi Tea went to great lengths to make sure the unique flavors of each blend are preserved; the research took over a year to make sure the flavor profile was balanced in the carbonated beverage. Rishi Marketing Director Jeffrey Champeau noted in an OnMilwaukee.com article that creating the carbonated tea on tap required "looking at the nuances in the herbs we're using and blending."

Even the temperatures at which each ingredient is steeped can differ. Some ingredients require hot extraction while others require cold. Although currently only served on tap , the success of the product in Milwaukee could determine whether or not Rishi moves forward with this carbonated tea idea to sell it by the bottle.

As Rishi Tea progresses into new markets with its tried and true loose leaf tea and new products, it's easy to see it is staying committed to its founder's vision of bringing the delicious flavors of tea from across the globe to the United States. Rishi has recognized quickly that while its loose leaf organic teas are impressive and well-loved by tea connoisseurs, there is a larger market for tea out there.

Rishi's innovations in high-quality tea bags and fun trends make its brand more accessible to the general public. When Conley joined the brand three years ago, she said, "I could see the possibility for the tea category and the tea segment." Conley commended the leadership at the company, noting, "We are all very collective in that we want to share the story of Rishi Tea."

Rishi Tea's fundamental understanding of tea and the consumer, coupled with innovation, is driving the growth of tea and helping people across the United States appreciate good tea in their everyday lives.

*   *

Across the pond, another company is working to bring authentic Asian teas to the German consumer.

Michael Decker and Felix Ilse have always been entrepreneurs at heart. They started as friends in high school, always having side hustles. Despite attending different universities, they managed to stay in touch and up to date on the startup world. After graduating, Decker and Ilse took a year off before working and traveled and studied in Taiwan and Argentina, respectively. During this year, it was their goal to launch a new business. They had great respect for physical products in a world where tech seemed to be all the rage. And once they got out of Germany and traveled the world, it hit them—the product they were going to launch was tea.

Because of Taiwan's rich tea history, during his travels, Decker was able to learn the benefits of tea—especially matcha—first-hand from monks. Meanwhile, across the globe in Argentina, his business partner Ilse was learning the traditions of mate. Using these experiences, Decker and his co-founder embarked on a journey to change the landscape of tea in Germany. They noticed from the start that tea was seen as old-fashioned and outdated in Germany. Coming home from their travels to Argentina and Taiwan, where tea traditions are so old, this seemed counterintuitive. But Decker and Ilse noticed it was the older generations that took tea in Germany, in contrast to the other countries they had visited in which everyone, young and old, took tea. They noticed an opportunity in Germany to seize a part of the tea market that had long been ignored: young people.

Together they founded Teatox, a German tea company that lies at the intersection of health and authenticity in tea. Decker said, "Teatox believes that ultra healthy teas do not have to taste bad; it's been about taste with health benefits from the beginning." This ethos is visible in all parts of Teatox's operations. Decker and Ilse have studied the intricacies of building tea blends straight from the source. With a name like Teatox, they balance their blends in ways that maximize consumer health benefits, but they do not forget about the consumer's enjoyment. Teatox understands that while consumers are drawn by the health benefits, they want their customers to experience "special moments while enjoying tea." They market their product so that customers purchase Teatox for the health qualities, but they keep repurchasing because the tea tastes good and is enjoyable, unlike similar tea detox products.

Another big distinction from their competition is Teatox's stand-out packaging. Noticeably more modern and cool than their competitors' packages, Teatox products come in simple stainless steel tins. Decker credits a large part of their success to their ability to catch the consumer's eye on the shelf.

From a young age, Decker was aware of the importance of enjoying tea. He remembers going to his grandparents' house and taking tea on Sundays after lunch. His grandmother would boil a pot of tea and offer him cookies or other sweets. Decker also notes that people in Germany typically seek out chamomile tea as a remedy to colds. Teatox, however, aims to be a tea used for general health, every day, not only when sick.

At the heart of Teatox's mission is "to change the way tea is seen." Decker and Ilse have had to change this market misconception that tea is only for sick days in order for Teatox to be successful and so far, they are succeeding. In fact, they will begin exporting their product to the United States in early 2018.

Although Germany is very different from the United States, one can draw parallels between how consumers in each country tend to view tea as something old and traditional. Teatox's mission of "changing the way tea is seen" is vital to reviving tea for Germany and should position the company well for its entry into the U.S. market.

Decker never thought tea would be the product that he and Ilse ended up launching. But their travels inspired them and they found an opportunity in the market they could not pass up. By offering a tea product that not only does good, but also tastes good, Decker and Ilse have been able to promote tea as part of everyday life, not just as a cold remedy. With its modern product packaging and an authentically inspired tea detox based on their own travels, Teatox has been able to be a part of a tea awakening in Germany and across the world.

Companies like Teatox and Rishi Tea are leveraging tea's rich traditions in their sourcing and innovation. They aim to break the mold by offering great quality and by distancing themselves from traditional, uninspired tea bags.

A perfect example of this idea of honoring traditional quality while also innovating is Taylor Drye's Mad Monk Tea in San Diego, California. Drye set up shop as a tea importer after spending what he calls "too much time" in the liquor industry. Mad Monk Tea is a tiny shop with limited hours and sells just 12 types of tea. Drye only sells the tea leaves to a small community of customers but happily sits down for tea with anyone who shops.

Drye takes pride in Mad Monk Tea. He says his company is an "innovator that stands on the shoulders of tradition." By honoring the tradition and quality of tea, he can leverage these associations for his brand and bring his product to the consumer in innovative ways.

*   *

SWEET ICED TEA

One of the most famous teas to catch on in the United States calls the South its home. Sweet. Iced. Tea. In the South, sweet iced tea is more than just a drink. As Allison Glock in *Garden & Gun* says, "Sweet tea isn't a drink, really. It's culture in a glass."

Historical fables claim that iced tea, in general, was created by accident by the Indian Tea Association at the St. Louis World's Fair in 1904. People at the fair weren't interested in a cup of piping hot tea during St. Louis' sweltering summer, so the tea association poured the piping hot tea over ice. Thus, an American icon was born!

Well, not so fast. Historians say this is not exactly true. While the Indian Tea Association may have served this cold beverage at the World's Fair, they didn't invent it. In fact, iced tea was started out a lot farther north.

Iced tea with a slice of lemon was actually a thing back in 1868, well before the World's Fair in 1904. A headline from the *Boston Journal* in the summer of 1868 said, "During the heated term there is nothing so invigorating as iced tea. A slice of lemon no thicker than a wafer placed in each tumbler adds to the relish." Notice, this headline came from Boston, in the North.

At the end of that same summer, down south, the *New Orleans Times* published a headline that read, "Iced tea with lemon juice is said to be a popular and healthy drink at the North."

You must be thinking, "Well, the north just invented iced tea, but the South added what's important: the sugar." That's just not the case. *Serious Eats* states that "from the very beginning, sweetening iced tea was a common practice, but it was left to the consumer's discretion. Lemon juice was mentioned more often than sugar in the early notices." Sugar was not necessarily a requirement, but it was added in the north before the South adopted iced tea at all.

Part of the reason iced tea was not as prevalent in the South early on is because of ice. It was very difficult to get ice down South until the 1920s, when ice machines were invented. But after this, sweet iced tea took off.

Although we can't exactly credit the South for originally adding the sugar, we can credit the South for originating the idea of "pre-sweetening" tea. Pre-sweetened tea required the sugar to be added when the beverage is still hot. That way, the ice dilutes the mixture only after it becomes concentrated with sugar. That's how true Southern sweet tea gets so sweet.

So if sweet tea or iced tea wasn't uniquely created in the South, why is it a part of Southern identity? Jeffrey Klineman has a unique opinion, expressed in a 2007 *Slate* article:

"The South reveres its traditions, and sweet tea is one of them. Dixie has had some embarrassments in its time: There's that whole Civil War thing, the whole Judge Roy Moore thing, that whole Naples, Fla., Swamp Buggy Queen thing, to name a few. Getting your nose rubbed in your own traditions too many times makes you cling to those that aren't, well, illegal."

And with that, I'll leave you with a nice suggestion. Head to the nearest Chick-fil-a, Waffle House, or McDonald's and get yourself a real Southern sweet tea.

CHAPTER 7

THIRD WAVE TEA

———

Tea has an image problem. Most people's experience of tea is through a tea bag: watery, weak, limp, unimpressive.

—JESSE JACOBS, FOUNDER OF
SAMOVAR TEA IN SAN FRANCISCO

Did you know millennials cannot afford housing because they buy too much avocado toast? NO?! Well, this probably isn't true, but according to Tim Gurner, an Australian millionaire, he "wasn't buying smashed avocado for $19 and four coffees at $4 each" when he was around the age of buying his first home.

The internet lashed out against these comments from Gurner during a "60 minutes" segment. Millennials were infuriated at his suggestion that their taste for expensive food and drink was why they found it hard to afford good housing, instead of low minimum wages and student debt, to name just a few reasons why young people may not be in the market for a new house.

Politics aside, the avocado effect isn't new. The *Washington Post* notes that when Starbucks was expanding its retail presence, many financial gurus blamed daily coffee habits for holding many Americans back from finding financial success. For example, "one personal finance guru, David Bach, even built an entire brand around it: You can use his 'Latte Factor Calculator' to see how much money you could save if only you'd forgo the daily coffee habit."

So why are innovations in food causing such a fuss? Well, according to Lindsay Drucker, a Goldman Sachs researcher, millennials value "experiences over big-ticket items like homes and cars." And a popular experience for young people is eating out. Millennials spend 44 percent of their food budgets on eating out, according to the Food Institute's 2014 analysis of U.S. Department of Agriculture data.

With these trends in mind, it's easy to recognize the explosion of innovations in food and drink industries—and tea is no different! Within the past few years we've seen the rise of the luxury single origin tea segment, cold brew tea, nitro brew tea, matcha lattes, turmeric-based teas, tea cocktails, green tea pills, and countless other trends in the tea market.

Most of these innovations are a part of what experts are calling "third wave tea." Just a few years behind the rise of third wave coffee, third wave tea shifts the focus of the tea market to its origins and purity.

Samovar Tea in San Francisco was at the edge of this third wave trend back in 2001, post-dot-com bubble. Samovar was founded by Jesse Jacobs to fulfill the mission of being a place "where we invite people to slow down, to inhabit the present moment, to disconnect in order to connect."

Samovar is a true third wave tea company that parallels the rise of third wave coffee. The analogy that many experts use to explain third wave coffee goes like this: If first wave coffee was Folgers, then second wave coffee was Starbucks. Starbucks is a place that made coffee more popular by providing customers with other additives (like syrups) to their coffee. And after Starbucks comes third wave. As described by *Fast Company's* Rebecca Greenfield, third wave coffee is "more concerned with process, and the coffee beans themselves: What's the best extraction method? A pour-over? A vacuum pump? What's the ideal water temperature? Oh! And if you aren't using a conical Burr grinder, what are you even doing with your life?" Third wave tends to focus more on the purity of the bean and a return to a simpler cup of coffee with fewer add-ins.

Greenfield applies this same theory to tea: Lipton is the first wave, Teavana—with all its herbal additives—is the second wave, and places like Samovar are the third wave.

*   *

My first taste of tea was probably when I was in the fifth grade, all thanks to second wave tea. I was in Colorado on vacation with my family. I am from Nebraska and lots of Nebraskans like to drive the seven to eight hours into the mountains during the summer to escape the humidity at home. The mountain air is so refreshing, it makes the drive worth it.

My family and I were in the small ski resort of Copper Mountain, getting ready to go on a hike. It was early in the morning and we stopped at the only coffee shop in town—it was called Camp Hale. We all ordered drinks, and of course, my little brother, little sister, and I got hot chocolates. We drank those in about two seconds, sucking down the sugar and chocolate instantly.

After getting our morning drinks, we purchased chairlift tickets. Now, my family is somewhat athletic, but we are not super outdoorsy. So for us, going on a hike was taking the chairlift up the mountain and walking down.

The chairlifts that ran in the summer were smaller and only held two people, so my dad and I were on a chairlift together. We boarded the lift and put down the safety bar. I always remember putting down the ski lift safety bar as the scariest part because it would shake the whole chair.

We were gliding up the mountain and my dad still had a full drink. He turned to me and asked, "Do you want some? I got a chai tea latte. It's really sweet; you'll like it."

Now, I was still really young, about 10 years old, and had never tried coffee or tea before. But I really wanted to try his grown-up drink, so I took a sip.

First off, I remember it being too hot. But I also remember it being too sugary and sweet, which is odd coming from fifth grade me. I have always had such a sweet tooth. But I think I found the chai latte too vanilla-like. I really like chocolatey-sweet things.

For my first impression of tea, I really didn't like it. In fact, I remember getting a slight headache. The chai tea latte was just so sugary to me, but it is one of my dad's greatest addictions.

My father was first introduced to chai tea lattes by a family friend. This friend had seen Tazo's Chai Tea concentrate on Oprah's Favorite Things segment and decided to give it to my father as a Christmas gift. My dad ended up loving the drink and to his delight, the beverage was offered at Starbucks in iced or hot form. Thank goodness.

Ever since I can remember, I have associated my father with chai tea. From a young age, he trained my brother, sister, and I how to order the perfect Venti Iced Chai from Starbucks. He always stresses that we need to tell the barista "six *full* pumps of the chai concentrate."

He's always so happy when they get his order right. He has a special way of mixing his drink by kind of swirling the cup. We always tried to copy him, but he would end up correcting our form, commenting, "It's all in the flick of the wrist." Donald was addicted to Starbucks' second wave, sugary tea.

But not everyone was as happy with Starbucks chai lattes as Donald. In fact, many people believe Starbucks harmfully appropriated chai lattes from Indian culture.

Anupy Singla, an American chef of Indian descent, was excited when she heard Starbucks was coming out with a chai drink, as it reminded her of learning to make the drink in Punjab, India, with her father's family. However, after tasting the drink, she was shocked by how unrepresentative it was of the authentic beverage. She was interviewed for an article on *Quartz* and said, "It makes me sad that people go and order this drink...thinking it's something associated with South Asia, and it's not."

The Starbucks version contains distinctly different flavors from many chai recipes in India. Even though chai recipes change by region and are not consistent, Starbuck's chai struck the wrong chord with many familiar with the Indian beverage. People commented that the drink was overall too sweet. In a *Quartz* article, Alisa Martinez, a Teavana spokeswoman, told *Quartz*, "The tea they sell is inspired by chai in India, and the sweetness and taste profiles were refined to match the customers' palate." Teavana is owned by Starbucks and is responsible for the tea flavors in the chai.

Nonetheless, Americans really love the second wave version of chai tea with all its added sugars.

Many second wave tea creations have come under similar cultural appropriation accusations. For example, in response to a *New York Times* article describing bubble tea, many readers pointed out the culturally insensitive way in which the newspaper introduced the tea.

One reader, Bo Hee Kim, commented:

> "The language used in this article, from 'exotic' to 'Far East' and the unappealing nature of the word 'blob' to describe

a drink well-known to many Asians and Asian-Americans unintentionally alienates this population from reading this article. It highlights otherness rather than uniqueness, defines familiarity through a nondiverse lens, and for me evokes the unpleasant feelings of being the kid in a nondiverse neighborhood bringing 'weird' lunches to school."

Readers didn't have as much of a problem with the beloved Taiwanese drink spreading to the states, but they took issue with the way it was being described—as if the *Times* had just "discovered" bubble tea from a faraway land.

When dealing with tea in the United States, it's important to note that all of the tea we enjoy comes from other countries and cultures and it's important to be cognizant and respectful of how we consume it, especially when it comes to innovations in second wave tea. Because this wave is characterized by adding sugars and other flavors to tea, it naturally deviates from many of the more traditional or authentic tea beverages beloved in various parts of the world.

*   *

While second wave tea may need to be more cautious of how it pays homage to the great teas of the world, third wave tea is about bringing back the simplicity of tea, with no add-ins. It refocuses on the purity of teas.

San Francisco's Samovar Tea takes a third wave approach with its focus on the process of harvesting and brewing tea and on the tea leaves themselves. As we now know, all tea comes from the same tea plant: *Camellia sinensis.* According to *Fast Company*, Samovar typically only has eight types of tea on the menu: "black, green, herbal, two types of chai, matcha, and two types of iced."

This simplified menu reflects Samovar's focus on bringing out the true flavor of teas. Many third wave enthusiasts believe tea does not need extra sweetening and flavoring. If brewed properly, the delicious flavors will come through without any extras.

Despite the simple menu, selecting which types of tea to put on the menu and brewing the tea is not a simple process. Lots of people compare tea to wine—there are so many different varieties and complex flavors. Just as there are wine sommeliers, being a tea sommelier is an actual job.

Chris Day is a dining room manager at Eleven Madison Park—a very fancy, three-Michelin-star restaurant in New York—and he started a tea program there in 2011. He and his suppliers of tea started realizing the benefits of third wave tea. "(We were) like wait a minute, we don't need to taint tea with anything. It's oolong tea. And see how great it is. That's kind of the next step."

Samovar shares a similar approach with Eleven Madison Park. However, it's not just Samovar's simple menu, focus on true tea flavors, and process that attracts me to this tea shop's concept. It's Samovar's mission that invites people to slow down.

In my mind, tea serves a different purpose than coffee. Although I love tea so much that I'm writing a book about it, I can't go a day without my cup of coffee. Coffee is utilitarian. I need it for the quick fix of caffeine and energy to start my day. Some people may use tea for its caffeine in an effort to be health conscious, but its lower caffeine content doesn't cut it for me.

So why do I still drink tea? Well for me, tea is about the experience; it's meant to be enjoyed. *Fast Company*'s Rebecca Greenfield agrees, stating, "Coffee is a convenience. Tea is enjoyed."

So where does this leave tea? If tea isn't a replacement for my cup of coffee, what is it? The challenge posed to companies from a consumer like me is that I don't always view tea as a substitute for my coffee. Third wave tea has realized this in ways that larger tea companies have not: Third wave tea is competing on experience.

Jacobs highlights the way that companies like Samovar have seized this opportunity: "Tea has an image problem. Most people's experience of tea is through a tea bag: watery, weak, limp, unimpressive." Companies like Samovar aim to flip the script by providing bold, yet simple, menus and a space to slow down and experience your tea.

*　*

Another key characteristic of third wave tea is its focus on the process of making a cup of tea. There are lots of intricate details to follow for steeping different varieties of tea. It can get really complex and many consumers, including myself, lose patience for this type of craftsmanship when it comes to everyday enjoyment.

Imagine a world where brewing the perfect cup of tea was as simple as the touch of a button. It's 7:01 a.m. and your alarm is beeping—Monday morning is a rude awakening.

But your morning routine just got a little sweeter. From the comfort of your bed, you can begin brewing your favorite cup of tea. Your senses are awakened by the aroma of your Japanese tea being prepared by your Teforia.

The Teforia is a "tea experience for the modern world." Teforia is a high-quality version of a Keurig, specifically for tea. *TechCrunch* describes the device as "an Internet-connected tea infuser that could brew the pre-packaged teas."

Teforia was launched in 2015 after two years of intensive development. The device is impressive. It boasts internet connectivity so that each blend can be brewed in just the right way.

Teforia sells its own blends in pods called "Sips." The pods even have radio-frequency identification tagging so the device knows how to properly brew each blend. The product is connected to an app that gets summaries of the flavors of each blend, and the app can also ask you questions to determine the optimal brewing process for your own blends when you're not using the "Sips" pods. There is even an online community via the app so tea lovers can share their favorite blends and brewing processes.

Allen Han founded the startup after being disappointed in his cups of tea at specialty coffee shops. Han worked in Seattle at the time when third wave coffee was sweeping the city. A coworker asked him to visit a new specialty coffee shop. Knowing Han did not drink coffee and was more of a tea fanatic, the coworker suggested, "They make a great cup of coffee, I'm sure they'll do something great with tea." After hearing this, Han told *Co.Design*, "I was pretty stoked, finally, someone's gonna make a great cup of tea!"

Needless to say, Han was disappointed. He got the same boring experience of basic tea in a paper cup. No hype, no craftsmanship. Why did coffee get all the limelight?

This was what Han calls his trigger point. "Where was my craft tea?" After being inspired by this experience, Han said, "I did a study around the business, and ritual, of tea. It's the second most drank beverage in the world after water! Even in the U.S., where consumers spent $30 billion coffee, they spent $27 billon on tea. That was a shocking number for me, because as a tea drinker, I thought it was in a minority in the U.S."

Like we have come to realize in this book, Han came to appreciate how big tea is around the world. And Han's product aims to capture the luxury aspect of this massive market.

However, in October of 2017, Teforia went bust. At $1,000, the tea infusers were overpriced for most consumers. The market was not ready to pay so much for a technology it did not quite understand.

When I first heard of Teforia, it was from a *TechCrunch* article poking fun at the startup going bust. The punchline was that it was obvious that a company that sells glorified Keurigs for $1,000 would go bust. The description of the article read, "Oh, no one wanted your $1,000 tea infuser? You don't say," accompanied by a cheeky meme.

I immediately thought this was funny. Of course no one was buying the tea infuser at that ridiculous price. The whole idea seemed so pretentious and it embodied a lot of the things I don't like about tea. The product pushed the narrative that in order to enjoy tea, it must be brewed perfectly. But who has time or money for that?

But after doing a little more research and hearing founder Allen Han's vision behind the product, I've warmed up to the idea. The product attempted to leverage its internet connectivity and expert design to make the tea experience easy for the end user while maintaining the integrity of the tea.

Teforia represents a larger trend in innovation in the kitchen appliance sector. It's cool to see tea being a part of that trend and conversation. While the market may not be ready for Teforia yet, its technology may well be part of the future of tea. Tea consumption has not changed much in the past 5,000 years, but with the rise of new technology, we may see more innovations like Teforia.

*   *

Through the examples of Samovar and Teforia, we have seen how third wave tea aims to get back to the basics—focusing on simplicity and purity of the infusing process. Although there is a refined focus on the process of infusing tea, that doesn't mean enjoying tea needs to become more complex. After all, the third wave is all about making tea simpler.

One way this is evident is in Samovar's design of its newest San Francisco storefront. Everything in the store is minimalistic and aims to "bring the focus on tea," says Jacobs.

Modern Living describes the new storefront saying, "You won't find 50 different varieties of green tea or herbal blends that resemble drinkable potpourri. In their place are precisely calibrated, tablet-controlled glass tea-brewing crucibles, made in Utah by Alpha Dominche, dispensing ready-made cups of impeccably sourced herbal, green, black and chai blends."

By removing other distractions, customers can focus on the taste of their tea. All of this is in an effort to make tea "fast, cheap, delicious, beautiful, potent," according to Jacobs. He doesn't want to replicate other tea houses that have endless varieties of tea, costing upwards of $15 for one pot. Instead, his goal is to "is to make tea become a daily habit."

Modern Living explains how he's going to reach his goal.

"Jacobs makes a compelling case: Like coffee, tea, he says, went through a colonial-era wave, suffered through a mass-marketed-crap wave, and is now primed to challenge coffee for caffeinated-morning supremacy, or at least offer a thoroughly convincing alternative. Samovar's cups are priced at $3-$5 and can be brewed in a few minutes, making them comparable in cash and wait time to a cup from Four Barrel or Blue

Bottle. Also key to tea's image makeover, Jacobs says, is a lack of consumer choice: the average teashop, he argues, offers 'too many choices. People are already overwhelmed; no one wants to choose something early in the morning.'"

By refocusing on the quality of the product without overwhelming the customer with too much choice or products that are too expensive, Jacobs is hoping he can make third wave tea catch on and become more of a norm.

But providing quality, economical tea isn't the only thing Samovar specializes in; the company also cares deeply about the experience it offers. Samovar's locations are mainly in California's Silicon Valley, a very competitive, cutthroat region. Samovar aims to serve as a safe haven from "the rat race," says *LigaStudios*. Samovar has become "appreciated by locals as an escape from the demands of a digitally demanding lifestyle."

Not only is third wave tea about making tea better tasting and more accessible, it's also about cultivating the experience; it's about giving people space to take a break, relax, and reconnect.

* *

G&T—GIN AND TEA

While most of third wave tea is about getting back to the simplicity of the tea leaves and making tea more accessible, third wave tea also encompasses cool, new innovations. From cold brewed tea to nitro brewed tea to matcha lattes to tea cocktails, or "tea-tails," third wave tea is full of exciting creations.

One of the new ideas that I can really get behind is tea cocktails. In this chapter's recipe, I want to highlight one of my favorites—the G&T, a twist on a classic.

Gin is a unique liquor. It has a refreshing, piney taste. And by simply adding tonic and a lime, you've got a great cocktail that stays fresh; it's not weighed down by fruity flavors.

Gin is also a controversial liquor. Some people hate the piney taste, others love it. There are countless *Buzzfeed* articles that explain how studies have found that people who like the taste of gin have psychotic characteristics.

The recipe I want to share with you is based off the old classic, but with an added ingredient: green tea.

Here's a list of what you'll need:

- 1.5 oz of gin
- 2 oz of chilled green tea (I use Rishi's Jade Cloud green tea. Shocker.)
- 3 oz of tonic

- a handful of ice cubes
- a large wine glass

Let's start by preparing the green tea, as this will take the longest. You'll want to start by boiling your water to around 180 degrees Fahrenheit. I use Rishi's Jade Cloud green tea, but any tea will do. I like to stick with a Chinese green tea, rather than a Japanese green tea (a Sencha tea, for example). Chinese green tea will give you more of a light, floral flavor. A Japanese green tea will be stronger, but more umami, which just doesn't sit right with gin, for me.

For this brew, I like to steep the tea leaves a full three minutes to get as much bold flavor as possible. I steep two tea sachet in about 6 to 8 ounces of water, as I normally make more than one G&T for friends (Don't drink alone, guys!). I try to make the tea a bit concentrated to pack a punch, so a strong green tea flavor comes out in the cocktail.

After steeping the tea a little on the longer side, place it in the fridge to chill. The colder the tea gets, the better, but it could take over 30 minutes. I'm usually in too much of a rush to plan out my beverage, so I let it sit as long as it takes to prepare the other components (I often end up adding hot tea because I have a huge lack of foresight).

While your tea is cooling, add your gin, tonic, and ice cubes to a large wine glass. Make sure you've got a glass big enough to handle all the liquid and ice. Big wine glasses tend to work well and look fancy.

After stirring the gin, tonic, and ice cubes, pour in your chilled green tea. Take a super artsy photo of your drinks, then cheers!

CHAPTER 8

TEA AND THE NEW GENERATION

———

Coffee's cool. Tea's not. Coffee's got George Clooney and Jean Dujardin; tea's got Johnny Vegas and an unnecessarily condescending knitted monkey. Coffee is James Dean lethargically drawing on a Marlboro he's slipped out of the packet he keeps rolled up in the sleeve of his white T-shirt. Tea is a greying dad in a fleece sitting in his Volvo Estate outside a school disco waiting for his daughter, winding down the window to unleash the sound of 'Lifted' by the Lighthouse Family as she approaches with her friends.

—VICE

The United States is not the only country where tea has an image issue. As it turns out, the kings of tea themselves, the British, can't even escape this problem.

For the first time in the history of the world, British tea consumption is now lower than coffee consumption. According to *Vice*, the British now "drink twice as much coffee as tea, with tea consumption falling by 19 percent since 2010." Someone pinch me. I must be dreaming. This is unreal. But, it's all too real. A country that prides itself on tea as the life-blood of their empire is now falling victim to coffee.

Like *Vice* notes, tea simply isn't cool anymore in Britain. And get this, the tea that's no longer cool is the classic British tea. It's just too boring. Now, *Vice* doesn't claim that matcha lattes from Japan and bubble tea from Taiwan aren't cool. In fact, *Vice* calls for more globally inspired tea to revive its popularity in Britain.

And the *Vice* article goes even further to shame anyone who refers to a cup of tea as a "cuppa." Now, I have definitely said "cuppa" in this book. But the truth is, I did not even know what "cuppa" meant until I did my research. While I was interviewing an expert, they referred to a cup of tea as a "cuppa." I had to later look up what it meant. Calling a cup a "cuppa" sounded weird to me at first, but then it kind of sounded comforting, like your grandma brewing you a cup of tea when you're sick.

But this "cuppa" tea narrative is exactly what tea needs to avoid if it's trying to be cool again. Who thinks being sick and your grandma taking care of you is cool?!

*   *

As shocking as this drop in tea consumption in Britain may be to me and other Americans, it's actually nothing new to the British. In fact, the British tea industry faced a similar predicament not too long ago after World War II. As illustrated by Erika Rappaport's research of the rise of coffee shops in Britain post-World War II in the 1960s, coffee's aura of rebellion, American-ness, and "cool" lured young people away from their national beverage.

In the "Tea in the United States" chapter, we learned that the Tea Council failed to turn around this shift in attitudes. Its "tea set" campaign with its corny slogans and lack of nuance did not impress its intended audience.

*   *

In the age of "third wave" coffee, we are seeing the same thing happen. As *Vice* notes, "The regeneration of coffee didn't come from nowhere, though; it was a careful exercise in branding and marketing, transforming coffee from a workday beverage you swig in a greasy spoon to a finessed premium product like fine wine or expensive cheese."

The coffee industry hasn't stopped innovating to fit the needs of its customers since it gained popularity for its rebellious vibes and counter-culture representation in Britain after World War II. New, exciting versions of the beverage keep coffee "cool," while the same old PG Tips tea bag with milk and sugar leave the young British consumer unimpressed.

While tea innovations have not been as visible to the British consumer, coffee innovations have been popping up everywhere, from cold brew coffees to nitro brew coffees and single origin, fancy coffee beans. Cute coffee houses promote a coffee-drinking community. Millennials flock there to do work using the free Wi-Fi, meet friends, or grab a cup on the go. What's worse, baristas at these hip coffee shops draw cute little hearts on everyone's latte foam. How is a boring tea bag at home supposed to compete with this Instagramable, Snapchat story-worthy aesthetic?!

There are three distinguishing factors of third wave coffee's success that third wave tea and tea in general are not managing as well: an appealing place for the beverage to be purchased and consumed, social media influence, and the success of second wave coffee.

First, coffee houses have been a huge factor in coffee's success. Coffee shops have become cool places to hang out, often equipped with free Wi-Fi to inspire working there. The physical environment of many third wave coffee shops is appealing to people who want a place to stay and do work or a convenient meeting place to sit and talk with friends. coffee houses have even become places of collaboration between students or professionals.

Although tearooms and teahouses exist in multitudes in the United States, they seem less accessible, whether that be because they are less ubiquitous or because of their atmosphere, which can come off as stuffy and unwelcoming. While coffee houses seem more accessible and casual, tearooms are often found in fancy hotels. Or, if they are not in a fancy hotel, they can sometimes feel intimidating to first-timers. I still get a little intimidated walking into a new tea shop!

The atmospheric differences in coffee houses and tearooms may play a role in the success of the coffee house. In addition, coffee houses tend to be more accessible in any given city. For example, in Washington D.C., I find a coffee house on almost every corner if I am trying to study. However, I have to search out and plan a little more for a trip to a tearoom.

Secondly, coffee has become extremely photogenic. Both latte art and the coffee houses themselves are attractive enough to share on social media. On Instagram alone, #coffee is tagged over 3.5 times more than #tea. If you think about it, for the world's most consumed beverage next to water, tea should have more tags on Instagram. But having a cup of tea in your home isn't as social media worthy as a $5 latte with a cute heart on it in an aesthetically pleasing coffee house.

Lastly, third wave coffee was primed by the success of second wave coffee. Second wave coffee is characterized by the addition of sugar and flavoring to coffee. This philosophy was championed by Starbucks, helping the company rise to the top, especially in the United States where Americans crave sugar and all things sweet. Because second wave coffee shops like Starbucks made coffee appealing to a wider audience by sweetening the normally bitter beverage, Americans developed a taste for coffee and many (me!) became addicted.

Coffee's wide acceptance in the United States during its second wave has undoubtedly helped the growth of third wave coffee. As a result of a growth in the base of coffee drinkers through second wave coffee, third wave coffee houses have a larger market of coffee drinkers to which they can sell their more upscale and expensive products.

* *

But not all is lost for tea. As we have learned, tea has its own "third wave." It may be smaller, and a little later than coffee's, but with innovations and continued support, tea can work to shake this association with "the greying dad in a fleece."

In addition, the tea industry can learn from third wave coffee. In terms of social media influence, third wave tea products themselves are getting more photogenic. For example, matcha lattes have milk on them and also can showcase latte art. In addition, the new products are worth sharing on social media out of sheer novelty. Cool tea-infused cocktails are irresistible to the share-happy millennial. Nitro brew teas at hip tea bars scream "put me on your Snapchat story." There are bottled teas infused with glitter that have over 250,000 tags with #chatime on Instagram.

In terms of creating a space as cool as a coffee house to enjoy tea, there are tearooms out there that have the similar aesthetics to coffee houses; they are just fewer and farther between. One *Guardian* article reacting to the drop in British tea consumption is titled "A little steep: why are there no tea bars in the UK?" It is harder for tea shops to stay in business because British consumers are used to drinking tea in the home and not paying a business for a simple cup of black tea with milk and sugar. However, tea rooms in the United States fare a little better because we do not have those strong associations of drinking tea in the home in the same way that the British do.

Although sometimes similar to a coffee house, tearooms tend to have a slightly different aesthetic, as discussed above. Sometimes this aesthetic can be off-putting or intimidating to consumers who do not have an in depth knowledge of tea. However, for me, sometimes these tearooms can be more relaxing than a normal coffee house because less people tend to be working at a tea house. Tearooms without wifi access are very calming and great places to talk with a friend. Tearooms can also serve as more of a learning experience. Because there are so many different types of tea, interactions with the tearoom employees can be very informative and helpful in selecting your tea.

Although these differences in atmosphere and aesthetics in tearooms may seem to put tea at a disadvantage, the idea of a tearoom being more relaxing or more of a learning experience can be leveraged to grow the popularity of tea. In fact, these tearooms greatly differentiate tea from coffee, especially in the regards of treating tea as an experience, rather than a beverage to fuel your work.

An alternative remedy for not having enough cool spaces to enjoy tea is infiltrating the menu of third wave coffee shops with tea offerings. We are already seeing this from second wave giants like Starbucks. With the acquisition of Teavana and later sale of Tazo, Starbucks made room for new Teavana products to shine through on its menu. This is a less capital-intensive way for tea to share the spotlight with coffee and even hope that some of coffee's "coolness" factor rubs off. For example, Starbucks' approach to tea uses Teavana's premium brand "to drive tea sales within Starbucks stores," said Charlie Cain of Building Oz. This approach has proven successful as "tea has consistently been among the fastest growing categories within Starbucks stores in the 4.5 years since the acquisition (of Teavana)."

*   *

Just as tea has borrowed ideas from third wave coffee in the past, by further exploring coffee culture and how tea culture can be modified to fit a new generation's needs and wants, the ancient art of tea will continue to be relevant with this new generation. As we've discussed in the earlier chapter "Third Wave Tea," many businesses have emphasized the opportunity third wave tea brings and are innovating to meet the needs and desires of young adult consumers.

At the heart of these changes is viewing tea as more than the leaves we steep. The new generation wants tea to be an experience—one that's new and exciting, full of aesthetic cups and tearooms.

*   *

BUBBLE TEA—A TAIWANESE FAVORITE

Bubble tea is a new phenomenon for American tea lovers. I remember the first time I tried bubble tea. It was about two and a half years ago at a farmers market. One of my friends had tried it before and wanted me to taste it. She was really excited!

The stand I was at only had one type of bubble tea. It was like a cold black tea with milk and little "bubbles" in it that were actually small pearls of tapioca. The tapioca pearls are called "boba." Bubble tea originated in Taiwan and is called boba tea there because of the tapioca pearls.

I took my first sip of the boba tea. It was cold and refreshing on that hot day.

I took my second sip. All of a sudden, a tapioca pearl shot into my mouth. I began to eat it. I thought to myself, "This is a different taste. I don't think I like tapioca," as I finished eating the chewy pearls.

My friend was shocked that I didn't enjoy the bubble tea as much as she did. Today, bubble tea has grown on me and I've started to like that tapioca flavor and no longer mind the chewy texture of the tapioca pearls. And bubble tea has also grown on the rest of the United States!

In the summer of 2017, *The New York Times* detailed the rise of bubble tea shops in New York City and their popularity. But some of the language the article used upset readers as it "unintentionally alienatc(d)" Asian-American culture," as one such reader, Bo Hee Kim, noted.

With the rising popularity of tea among young people (87 percent of millennials drink tea according to the Tea Association of the United States), bubble tea shops are popping up across the United States. Borrowing from a Taiwanese tradition that started 30 years ago, bubble tea has become a trend in the United States.

Bubble tea was invented on a whim, when a tea shop owner in Taiwan poured tapioca pearls from her pudding into a glass of iced Assam tea. The rest is history!

Today, there are many varieties of bubble tea. You can add matcha tea or experiment with different flavors of "bubbles." You are no longer limited to just tapioca if you don't like the flavor!

One of the ways that bubble tea shop owners are marketing and spreading the love of bubble tea is through college students. Many Asian or Asian-American college students are familiar with the Taiwanese bubble tea and introduce it to their friends. Bubble tea shop owners promote to these students and college campuses hoping that those familiar with the Asian beverage's background will spread it to their non-Asian college friends. This marketing strategy may be oddly specific, but it's working! In fact, this is how I discovered and tried my first bubble tea.

For many Americans, bubble tea is one of those new tea trends that is super aesthetic. Instagramming a picture of your refreshing boba tea is irresistible. Although you can definitely make your own boba tea, the process is long and difficult. There are so many boba shops popping up that going out and buying your own is becoming more and more convenient.

If you've never tried a bubble tea or boba tea, it's time to hop on the bandwagon, head over to the nearest boba shop, and sample this delicious Taiwanese beverage.

CHAPTER 9

STEVEN SMITH

—

What Starbucks did for coffee, craft brewers did for beer and artisanal vintners did for wine, Mr. Smith did for the Tao of tea.

—SAM ROBERTS OF *THE NEW YORK TIMES*

It was a Wednesday afternoon and I was walking back to my apartment. I was scrolling through notifications on my phone when I saw a *Wall Street Journal* notification that Starbucks Coffee had sold one of it tea brands, Tazo.

As someone writing a book about tea, I immediately scrolled through my phone and started finding other articles about the divestiture. My father even forwarded me an article about the sale.

It turned out that, after 18 years, Starbucks was ready to sell its beloved Tazo for $384 million to Unilever.

I first interacted with the Tazo brand thanks to my dad's chai tea addiction. The sweet chai flavor came from a Tazo-branded syrup. However, Tazo is much more than that.

When Starbucks first acquired the brand in 1999, it was worth $8.1 million. In its 18 years of ownership, Starbucks achieved massive growth with the brand, earning over 47 times return on the investment. Starbucks achieved this mainly due to its expansion into the retail space, with Tazo tea bags in grocery stores, K-cups, and bottled ready-to-drink teas. Tazo was the first Starbucks expansion into the tea segment. After increasing the value of the Tazo brand to $1.4 billion, Howard Schultz, longtime CEO and chairman of Starbucks, realized how profitable tea could be for the brand.

* *

While it took time for Starbucks to realize how profitable tea can be even for a coffee shop, Steven Smith has been enthralled with the power of tea for the majority of his professional life. Described by Entrepreneur.com as "a serial entrepreneur who won't take yes for an answer," Smith has been building new tea brands all his life, continuing to innovate and take risks in the industry despite multiple startup success stories.

Smith is behind the brand Tazo and many others, including Stash and Steven Smith Teamaker. "In tea, Steve has found his medium," comments Dave Leger, director of production for Steven Smith Teamaker.

Smith's first project was Stash. He joined the company, which originally sold herbs, in 1971. At the time, Celestial Seasonings was one of the only tea brands selling herbal infusions. Smith wanted to break into this segment with Stash, but at a higher price point. Smith began combining herbs from Stash with loose leaf tea. He recalls, "I hadn't been to China or India. I knew nothing about tea. But it worked."

Smith was also ahead of the curve on third wave tea. Back in the '90s, Smith was already exploring the idea of higher quality teas. He recalls, "If you had the best raw materials, you could create a super-premium product and charge even more. Nobody was doing that."

In fact, a lot of the tea inventions we take for granted today come from Smith's ideas. Bottled iced tea? Smith. As Entrepreneur. com notes, "Before Snapple bottled its first blend, before Honest Tea pushed the envelope with a lightly sweetened juice product, a first iteration of that beverage launched Tazo."

Well, what about the idea that tea evokes emotions? He's been there, done that. When Tazo launched in 1994, all the teas were named after emotions they should evoke: For example, names like Awake, Zen, and Calm "didn't tell you what was in them, but rather how they were supposed to make you feel," notes Entrepreneur.com.

With Tazo tea, Smith was really the first innovator in the industry to sell tea at a higher price and to a niche market. In the beginning, one box of Tazo tea cost $4.49. "Not bad," I thought to myself, but apparently, back in the '90s, that was ridiculous. Industry experts doubted Smith could sell his tea at $4.49 when brands like Celestial Seasonings sold their similar products at $1.99.

Smith had many haters.

"When Tazo first came out, I really thought it was bullshit," Mo Siegel, a founder of Celestial Seasonings, admits. "It was like a screenplay somebody had written. It was cute and well done, but it seemed totally invented. But he moved it around to where it became more mainstream."

Eventually, Tazo needed more money to keep scaling and Smith was in a tough place. He sold Tazo to Starbucks in 1999. He was involved with the brand at Starbucks until 2006, but then left because his new ideas for the brand were not being utilized. Smith recalls, "Everything I'd suggest, they'd say, 'Good idea, but we don't know how to scale it.'"

From 1999 to 2012, after 13 years in the tea industry with Tazo, Starbucks had weakened competing brand Teavana. In 2012, Teavana surrendered to Starbucks and was acquired for $620 million, the largest acquisition in Starbucks' history. Since the acquisition, Starbucks has focused on Teavana in an effort to serve a more premium tea experience to customers. Current CEO Kevin Johnson notes that the transition to Teavana "supports our strategy to elevate the premium tea experience for our customers." Starbucks effectively put the Tazo brand on the back burner in an effort to elevate Teavana into an even more premium category.

When I hear Teavana, I think of free samples in the mall and unwanted upselling. I remember the first time I went into a Teavana store. I was in the fourth grade and at the mall with one of my best friends; we were accompanied by my mom. Typically, my mom would not let me go into the Teavana store, either because we were in a rush or she just wanted to see other stores. However, because my friend and I were "hanging out" and shopping, she let us go in this time.

We tried the fruitiest herbal, pink tea ever. And we loved it. So naturally, the Teavana sales representatives managed to upsell us $50 and we left the store with not only the loose leaf tea, but also "sugar crystals" for sweetening the tea and a brewing tea pot contraption. Now I see why my mom never let me go in that store! The tea itself was expensive, but the upselling was even more detrimental to my bank account.

Now, this Teavana trip happened before Starbucks acquired the brand. Shortly after the acquisition in 2012, Starbucks announced it would close all Teavana retail locations. Looking back, I can now understand this move as very strategic. The stores were profitable, but gave off the wrong brand image for Starbucks.

Starbucks acquired the loose leaf brand to create a more upscale experience for its customers in its coffee shops. Teavana's strongest brand association was the quality of its loose leaf tea. Starbucks was looking to leverage this in its own coffee shops. However, the Teavana retail locations in the malls did not exactly scream premium or quality to many customers.

To me, a Teavana store is like the Bath & Body Works for tea. Bath & Body Works has an overwhelming amount of products and an overwhelming amount of headache-inducing smells. Teavana also has a huge product selection and quite a cloud of smells. Similar to my Teavana experiences, Bath & Body Works also has retail locations mainly in low quality, indoor shopping malls. Because of these similarities, I found it hard to see Teavana as a premium brand. Although

I recognize the higher quality of its products, its retail locations and store vibes did not live up to that standard.

Starbucks also recognized this. Teavana has great products, but its shopping mall retail locations did not always reflect this premium brand image Teavana had the potential to embody. Starbucks also realized Teavana had growth potential elsewhere and in other business models. Therefore, in July of 2017, Starbucks announced it would close the remaining 379 Teavana stores.

Strategically relevant to growing the premium brand image of Teavana teas in Starbucks, the decision to close Teavana stores is salient to the poor performance of shopping malls across the country. Credit Suisse predicts between 20 percent and 25 percent of U.S. malls will close in five years. Both problems with brand image and the decline of retail malls in the United States culminated in Starbucks' decision to close all Teavana retail locations.

With Starbucks' acquisition of Teavana in 2012, Tazo took a backseat. Tazo tea became a brand focused on tea bag sales in retail locations, while Teavana prominently filled the back counters of every Starbucks nationwide. Teavana was the base for successful Shaken Iced Teas, endorsed by Oprah Winfrey with her "Signature Chai," along with hot tea favorites like Emperor's Jade Cloud green tea bags. Starbucks has seen a "lift in revenue generated by the sale of handcrafted tea beverages in Starbucks retail stores driven in large part by the very strong customer response to the launch of Teavana branded Shaken Iced Tea and Teavana Tea Lattes," per Starbucks CEO Howard Schultz in January of 2015.

Fast forward to 2017 and Starbucks is ready to unload its investment in Tazo. Despite being Starbucks' second-tier tea brand, Unilever is happy to purchase the Tazo brand. Starbucks has stabilized its tea business, which now accounts for over 10 percent of sales and is ready to say goodbye to Tazo to the sweet tune of $384 million.

Unilever already has a wide tea portfolio, including Lipton, PG Tips, and Pure Leaf. Unilever is a CPG (consumer packaged goods) giant, selling everything from personal care to packaged food and beverages. Recently, under CEO Paul Polman, Unilever has focused on changing consumer behavior in the CPG industry by acquiring new, niche brands and focusing on sustainability.

Unilever's acquisition of Tazo is reflective of this strategy. Compared to some of its other tea brands like Lipton and PG Tips, Tazo is more of a niche brand. While Lipton and PG Tips largely focus on cost efficiencies in black tea, Tazo focuses on variety and quality. Tazo's website states "our tea buyers travel to origin countries regularly to taste and select some of the world's finest-quality teas," stressing the importance of quality in its leaves.

Kees Kruythoff, president of Unilever North America, notes that Tazo's "strong appeal to millennials...is a perfect strategic fit for our US portfolio. . . . Tazo's solid position in the fast-growing specialty tea segment, coupled with Unilever's tea expertise, presents a fantastic growth opportunity." With this acquisition, Unilever is buying into the emergence of niche tea brands in an effort to compete with the growing strength of smaller tea brands and appeal to changes in consumer behavior.

*   *

Thanks to businesses like Tazo, the foundation for the rise of third wave tea was laid back in the 1990s. The idea of going after a niche market with higher quality tea at a higher price originated with these tea brands that we now consider second wave. The idea that tea can have quality and be pricey translated well to second wave tea. And a brand like Tazo was perfect for the market that Starbucks wanted to capture at the time.

Now that we have phased through second wave tea, the world is ready for third wave tea. Just as Smith was able to help create and build this second wave of tea, he is also a part of the vision for third wave tea.

After selling Tazo and working for Starbucks on the Tazo brand until 2006, Smith took a yearlong break in France, but he couldn't stay away from tea for long.

While in France, Smith was inspired by artisans there making cheese, breads, and chocolates that were true to their French culture and heritage. He realized that his earlier tea brands were lacking this tradition. He returned to the tea industry with a new idea centered on tea being authentic.

With this new mission, Smith created Steven Smith Teamaker. In this tea line, Smith focuses on not only quality, but also on authenticity in his sourcing of the leaves. For example, Entrepreneur.com noted that this is reflected in teas "with names such as Mao Feng Shui, an amalgam of the connoisseur-level tea Mao Feng and the widely known Chinese phrase feng shui, the art of site orientation."

He traveled the world sampling different teas and blends to cultivate his understanding of tea origins and traditions. *The Oregonian* reports that "at one sip, Smith could tell which part of the world a tea came from and often which plantation had produced it." Smith's journey would shape a new wave of tea.

*   *

Steven Smith is the man responsible for many of the tea innovations we see in the United States. Unfortunately, in 2015, Smith passed away from liver cancer.

The New York Times notes that "what Starbucks did for coffee, craft brewers did for beer and artisanal vintners did for wine, Mr. Smith did for the Tao of tea." His work will be remembered and will remain critical in the world of tea and beverages for years to come.

This shuffling around of tea brands reflects a reaction to a larger trend in the tea industry, the emergence of "third wave tea." The coffee industry has seen it in third wave coffee. The beer industry has seen it with the rise of craft beers. Like Unilever notes in their grand strategy, consumer behavior has changed. What Smith noticed back in the '90s with Tazo tea, larger companies are just starting to realize. Consumers are demanding quality in their products, and third wave tea reflects this shift. While the big box brands like Lipton and PG Tips may never die, they must remain vigilant of these smaller tea companies focused on single origin blends, authenticity, sustainability, and quality. To supplement their portfolios, larger consumer product companies and coffee chains are acquiring more quality-focused brands to deliver to consumers.

While larger companies may be acquiring what we now consider second wave brands, they are doing so to react to the demand from consumers for enhanced experiences. New third wave companies are emerging to fill this niche void at a deeper level, going beyond the Tazo's and Teavana's of the second wave world. These third wave tea companies take quality even more seriously than did the second wave and add an element of source authenticity.

Steven Smith Teamaker is just one example of a tea company returning to a deeper authenticity. *The Oregonian* notes, "Smith's success inspired dozens of other high-end tea startups, elevating consumer standards and expectations."

*   *

TEA TASTING

In his early days, Smith propelled Tazo tea to the top by focusing on unique flavors in tea. This fascination with unconventional flavor combinations continued throughout his life.

Portland Monthly notes that Smith's most recent experiments included "scenting teas in whiskey, bourbon, and rum barrels, and creating a Portland-cool smoked tea." Commenting on the experiments, Smith said, "A lot of what we do here doesn't make any sense from the outside. It's the kind of stuff Tazo would call 'unscalable.'"

In honor of Smith's spirit of innovation and thirst for quality, for this last tea recipe, I am going to suggest a pilgrimage to Smith's tea holy land.

Even after his death, his family carries on his last business, Steven Smith Teamaker, in Portland, Oregon. Although his teas are available through retail and online, there are three tasting rooms worldwide—two in Portland and one in South Korea.

I've never been to any of the tasting rooms, but oh boy, it would be a dream to visit one.

CONCLUSION

———

Tea is more than the leaves we steep.

—HANNAH EVERETT

When I started out writing this book, I knew that I loved tea. My tea experiences had developed from a sip of chai on a chairlift in Colorado to a tasting room in Hangzhou, China, with British tea time with Ouma and Tea Nights on Alex's couch in between. And I had this one line stuck in my head, that "tea is more than the leaves we steep."

So I set out to write a book to find out more about how my personal experiences with tea fit into the bigger picture of the tea industry and tradition as a whole. And through this process, in each interview I conducted and each article I read, I kept finding a common thread: There was something *more* to tea.

Across continents, cultures, and generations, I kept finding my own story in the stories of others. From Mrs. Raj and Mr. Ma to Alex and Steven Smith, we all had taken a sip and felt something, something that connected us.

So listen up, Americans. Tea is not just a word squished into the corner of a chalkboard in a shop designed for the coffee lover, it's not simply an object colonists dumped in the Boston Harbor for attention, and it isn't only a source of caffeine for your Monday morning blues. Tea is *so much more.*

Tea is fundamentally an experience shaped by how we chose to enjoy the product. As evident by all of the people in this book, there are many different ways to enjoy tea, each just as special as the other. We have seen that tea can be used to slow down and take a break from work, like in India. Or tea can be used to show hospitality, as in Afghanistan where tea plays an especially important role in welcoming guests.

We have learned that all types of tea play a role in life. From the common-place PG Tips in England for an afternoon tea to the specialty loose leaf blends supplied by Rishi Tea in the United States, quality of tea is important but not everything.

So wake up, and grab a cup of coffee if you really have to—I'll understand. But don't sleep on tea. As the rise of third wave tea sweeps the United States, tea has begun to move from the corner of the chalkboard in the coffee house and take center stage in its own tea shop or become a larger part of the coffee house's business.

As we think about growing the base of American tea drinkers with third wave tea, we must not forget the value to be unleashed beyond the leaves and in the experience of drinking tea.

ACKNOWLEDGMENTS

Throughout my journey in creating this book, I was blessed with the opportunity to speak with many different people in the tea industry. I also got to sit down with amazing individuals that have had unique experiences with tea. Each conversation brought a better understand of tea and added to the rich experiences I have had with tea. Here is a list of the individuals that made this book possible:

Jessica Conley (Head of Hospitality at Rishi Tea)
Gail Gastelu (Editor in Chief of the Tea House Times)
Erika Rappaport (Professor of History at University of California Santa Barbara, Author of *A Thirst for Empire: How Tea Shaped the Modern World*)
Michael Decker (CEO and Founder of TeaTox)
Isabella Perera (Sales Representative at Just Paper and Tea)

Carol Benedict, PhD. (Professor of History at
Georgetown University)

I would also like to thank the following tea enthusiasts for
providing me with key insights into the mind of the consumer.

Hung Ma (Taiwanese tea enthusiast)
Jawed Sakhi (Afghan tea enthusiast)
Geetha Raj (Indian tea enthusiast)
Bridget Bingham
Alex Rimoldi
Field Daniel
Angela Caprio

Finally, I would like to thank Mary Caprio and Sarah Wright
for providing me with guidance and support in the creation
and editing of my book. I would also like to thank New
Degree Press, Brian Bies, and Eric Koester for making all of
this possible.

ENDNOTES

———

INTRODUCTION

1. Gebely, Tony. "Tea Tastes in 2017: A Forecast from 7 Experts on World of Tea." *World of Tea*, Eggs and Toast Media, LLC, 26 Apr. 2017, worldoftea.org/2017-tea-trends/.

2. Terazono, Emiko. "Financial Times Young Americans turn to tea." *Financial Times*, A Nikkei Company, 17 Mar. 2015, www.ft.com/content/97200586-cbe7-11e4-beca-00144feab7de.

3. Greenfield, Rebecca. "Giving Tea The Blue Bottle Treatment." *Fast Company*, Fast Company, 18 Apr. 2017, www.fastcompany.com/3041152/giving-tea-the-blue-bottle-treatment.

CHAPTER 1

1. "Assam, India—Assam Teas." *RateTea*, ratetea.com/region/assam/14/.

CHAPTER 2

1. "Origin of Tea." India Brand Equity Foundation, www.teacof-feespiceofindia.com/tea/tea-origin.

2. Bhagat, Chetan . "Where is our chai? Among other national crises this one is equally dire: A flood of mediocre machine tea." Times of India Blog, 25 Nov. 2017, blogs.timesofindia.indiatimes.com/The-underage-optimist/where-is-our-chai-among-other-national-crises-this-one-is-equally-dire-a-flood-of-mediocre-machine-tea/.

3. "Why I Am Proud To Be A Tea Addict." Chai Wallahs of India, 24 Apr. 2015, chaiwallahsofindia.com/2015/04/proud-tea-addict/.

4. Winsby, Amelia. "A Psychologists Honest Review of 7 Cups of Tea." Time2Track Blog, Time 2 Track, 26 Sept. 2017, blog.time2track.com/a-psychologists-honest-review-of-7-cups-of-tea.

CHAPTER 3

1. "CURRENT SITUATION AND MEDIUM TERM OUTLOOK FOR TEA." www.fao.org, Food and Agricultural Organization of the United Nations, Jan. 2012, http://www.fao.org/fileadmin/templates/est/COMM_MARKETS_MONITORING/Tea/Documents/IGG_20/12-CRS7-CurrentSit_01.pdf.

2. Admin. "Tea vs Coffee Import Superpowers." Dominion Tea, Dominion Tea, 17 Jan. 2017, blog.dominiontea.com/2015/05/21/tea-vs-coffee-imports-superpowers/.

3. "Hospitality Afghanistan Culture." About Afghanistan Culture, About Afghanistan, 2011, www.about-afghanistan.com/hospitality-afghanistan-culture.html.

4. "Bill and Bob's Excellent Afghan Adventure." Bill and Bob's Excellent Afghan Adventure, 3 July 2008, billandbobsadventure.blogspot.com/2008/07/chai.html.

5. "TEA AND HOSPITALITY IN AFGHANISTAN PART I." Afghan Culture Unveiled, 10 Oct. 2013, www.afghancultureunveiled.com/humaira-ghilzai/afghancooking/2013/10/tea-and-hospitality-in-afghanistan.html.

6. Smith, Oliver. "Mapped: The countries that drink the most tea." *The Telegraph*, Telegraph Media Group, 9 May 2017, www.telegraph.co.uk/travel/maps-and-graphics/tea-consumption-per-capita/.

CHAPTER 4

1. Whitehead, Nadia. "High Tea, Afternoon Tea, Elevenses: English Tea Times For Dummies." *NPR*, NPR, 30 June 2015, www.npr.org/sections/thesalt/2015/06/30/418660351/high-tea-afternoon-tea-elevenses-english-tea-times-for-dummies.

2. Aggeler, Madeleine. "The Origins Of The Kermit Sipping Tea Meme." *Bustle*, Bustle, 22 Dec. 2017, www.bustle.com/p/what-is-the-kermit-sipping-tea-meme-a-history-of-this-muppets-shade-69015.

3. "Kermit te frog." *Memegenerator.net*, memegenerator.net/Kermit-Te-Frog, Image.

CHAPTER 5

1. "UPASI TEA RESEARCH FOUNDATION." *UPASI TEA RESEARCH FOUNDATION (TRF)*, www.upasitearesearch.org/tea-quality-parameters.

2. Brickman, Sophie. "The 8 Drinks That Made My Career: Jim Meehan." First We Feast, First We Feast, 20 Oct. 2016, firstwefeast.com/drink/2012/11/jim-meehan-pdt-8-career-changing-drinks/.

3. Onion, The. "Relaxing Tea Better Fucking Work." *Local*, Local.theonion.com, 15 Sept. 2016, local.theonion.com/relaxing-tea-better-fucking-work-1819579209.

CHAPTER 6

1. History.com Staff. "Boston Tea Party." *History.com*, A&E Television Networks, 2009, www.history.com/topics/american-revolution/boston-tea-party.

2. "The Reason Britain Loves Tea." Great Big Story, www.greatbigstory.com/stories/why-the-brits-love-tea.

3. History of Indian Tea, www.indiatea.org/history_of_indian_tea.

4. "Tea Exporters Association Sri Lanka." Tea Exporters Association, teasrilanka.org/aboutus.

5. Lori Fredrich Senior WriterE-mail author | Author bioMore articles by Lori Fredrich. "Drink this now: Rishi Craft Brew." OnMilwaukee.com, 31 Jan. 2017, onmilwaukee.com/dining/articles/drink-this-now-rishi-craft-brew.htmlas.

6. "Our Mission." *Rishi Tea*, www.rishi-tea.com/aboutus.

7. Moss, Robert. "Why "As Southern as Sweet Tea" Isn't Very Southern at All." Serious Eats, www.seriouseats.com/2016/12/sweet-tea-origin-story-history-south.html.

8. "Tea in Sri Lanka: Travelers take sips of history." CNN, Cable News Network, 11 Feb. 2015, www.cnn.com/travel/article/sri-lanka-tea-experiences/index.html.

9. "Scotland's Legacy in Sri Lanka." *Scotland*, 1 Apr. 2015, www.scotland.org/features/scotlands-legacy-in-sri-lanka.

CHAPTER 7

1. Judkis, Maura. "Perspective | Don't mess with millennials' avocado toast: The Internet fires back at a millionaire." *The Washington Post*, WP Company, 15 May 2017, www.washingtonpost.com/news/food/wp/2017/05/15/dont-mess-with-millennials-avocado-toast-the-internet-fires-back-at-a-millionaire/?utm_term=.be91edff8255.

2. Calfas, Jennifer . "Avocados Are Why You Can't Afford a Home, Millionaire Says | Money." Time, Time, 15 May 2017, time.com/money/4778942/avocados-millennials-home-buying/.

3. Greenfield, Rebecca. "Giving Tea The Blue Bottle Treatment." Fast Company, Fast Company, 18 Apr. 2017, www.fastcompany.com/3041152/giving-tea-the-blue-bottle-treatment.

4. "Samovar Q & A With Founder, Jesse Jacobs." Samovar Tea, www.samovartea.com/about/.

5. Kohli, Sonali. "No, Starbucks' Chai Tea Latte is not real

chai." *Quartz*, Quartz, 20 Feb. 2015, qz.com/346582/
no-starbucks-chai-tea-latte-is-not-real-chai/.

6. "Our Readers Call Us Out Over Bubble Tea. They Are Right."
The New York Times, The New York Times, 17 Aug. 2017,
www.nytimes.com/2017/08/17/reader-center/our-readers-
call-us-out-over-bubble-tea-they-are-right.html.

7. Lynley, Matthew. "$1,000 tea infuser startup Teforia shuts
down." TechCrunch, TechCrunch, 27 Oct. 2017, techcrunch.
com/2017/10/27/1000-tea-infuser-startup-teforia-shuts-
down/?utm_medium=TCnewsletter.

8. Wilson, Mark. "Teforia Is Much More Than A Keurig For
Tea." Co.Design, Co.Design, 2 May 2017, www.fastcodesign.
com/3052743/teforia-is-much-more-than-a-keurig-for-tea.

9. Marx, Rebecca Flint. "Fancy Contraptions, Minimalist
Storefront, and Chinese Production-It's Not the Apple Store,
It's Third Wave Tea." San Francisco Magazine | Modern
Luxury, 1 July 2014, www.modernluxury.com/san-francisco/
story/fancy-contraptions-minimalist-storefront-and-chi-
nese-production-its-not-the-appl.

10. Magazine, LigaStudios. "The Rise of Third-Wave Tea."
LigaStudios Magazine, 18 Feb. 2016, www.ligastudios.com/
industries/tea-houses-jugetsudo-samovar-manuteefaktur.

CHAPTER 8

1. Staff, VICE. "We Asked Some Experts How to
Make Drinking Tea Cool Again." *Vice*, 15 Apr.

2016, www.vice.com/en_uk/article/bnkdg4/
we-asked-people-how-to-make-tea-cool-coffee.

2. Cain, Charlie. "Why Starbucks is closing 379 Teavana stores
    as specialty tea sales rise." *Building Oz, Inc.*, 5 Aug. 2017,
    buildingoz.com/2017/07/31/why-starbucks-is-closing-379-
    teavana-stores-as-specialty-tea-sales-rise/.

CHAPTER 9

1. Danny. "Starbucks to Sell Tazo Brand for $384 Million."
    QSR magazine, 2 Nov. 2017, www.qsrmagazine.com/news/
    starbucks-sell-tazo-brand-384-million.

2. Bolton, Dan. "Teavana Trumps Tazo at Starbucks." World
    Tea News, Penton, 26 Jan. 2015, worldteanews.com/news/
    teavana-trumps-tazo-starbucks.

3. "Unilever to Acquire TAZO® Brand from
    Starbucks." Business Wire, 2 Nov. 2017, www.busi-
    nesswire.com/news/home/20171102006644/en/
    Unilever-Acquire-TAZO%C2%AE-Brand-Starbucks.

4. Schoenfeld, Bruce. "How the Serial Entrepreneur Behind
    Tazo Tea Brews Up Success." Entrepreneur, 24 Jan. 2012,
    www.entrepreneur.com/article/222578.

5. Oregonian/OregonLive, Richard Read | The. "Portland
    tea savant Steven Smith, co-Founder of Tazo, Stash and
    Smith Teamaker, dies at 65." OregonLive.com, 23 Mar.
    2015, www.oregonlive.com/business/index.ssf/2015/03/
    steven_smith_tea_tazo_stash_st.html.

6. Roberts, Sam. "Steven Smith, a 'Marco Polo' of American

Tea, Dies at 65." *The New York Times*, The New York Times, 25 Mar. 2015, www.nytimes.com/2015/03/26/business/steven-smith-tea-explorer-dies-at-65.html.

7. Tepler, Benjamin. "The Story Behind Steven Smith's Obsession with Tea." *Portland Monthly*, 3 Nov. 2014, www.pdxmonthly.com/articles/2014/11/3/the-story-behind-steven-smiths-obsession-with-tea-october-2014.

90923872R00101

Made in the USA
Lexington, KY
17 June 2018